BEYOND LISTENING

To Jon,
Thank you for being a part of my journey to create this book of my heart.

BEYOND LISTENING

BRIDGING THE COMMUNICATION GAP BETWEEN PARENTS AND TEENS

LISA JASS

NEW DEGREE PRESS

BEYOND LISTENING

BRIDGING THE COMMUNICATION GAP

BETWEEN PARENTS AND TEENS

ISBN   978-1-63676-796-3 *Paperback*

              978-1-63676-797-0 *Kindle Ebook*

              978-1-63676-798-7 *Ebook*

"Sometimes being a good parent is admitting that you weren't a perfect parent."

—COLLEEN FERRARY BADER

In loving memory of Mark Takkinen and John Link, two great mentors whose advice I still hear in my head. I am forever grateful for their guidance and friendship. I will share my stories of them forever.

To mom and dad, who opened their home to many teens and raised two children who not only love them but like them too.

CONTENTS

INTRODUCTION

———

One day, I walked into Coach Takk's office. He took one look at me and asked, "What's wrong?" I immediately burst into tears. "I have no idea what I'm crying about," I said to him. He just leaned back in his chair, crossed his arms over his chest, and waited. I honestly don't remember what the issue was right now, but there were so many moments like that. Sometimes he would catch me grinning, and he would want to know the good stuff too, and he would wait for me to tell him, even if I might be embarrassed. He could read my emotional grid. He would just listen, and when needed or wanted, he would offer advice, a kind word, his shoulder to cry on, or a place to laugh out loud. He would often "see" what I wasn't saying. He spent the time to really get to know his students, and he let us get to know him too.

The funny thing about the beginning of my friendship with Mark Takkinen, lovingly known by everyone as Coach Takk, is that we both told the story pretty much the same way. He became the head football coach at the end of my sophomore year of high school, where I had been working as a student athletic trainer since the second week of my freshman year. I thought he was a loud bully, and he thought I was an entitled little bitch who thought I knew everything.

It didn't take either of us long to realize that we were mistaken, but we both loved to tell the story of our first impressions.

Coach Takk quickly became my mentor, my friend, a second father, and my go-to person when I needed advice or a shoulder to cry on. His family became a second family to me, and I shared many holidays with them. I had two of his children in my English class and also attended his daughter's wedding.

In many ways, engaging with a teen is like walking into a minefield where any wrong move can lead to a blowup. Coach Takk was so good at diffusing these situations because he took the time to understand each of us. I know his approach impacted how I interact with teenagers. I wanted to have that type of relationship with my students, and I wondered if this was something all of us could learn from. What I found has changed the way I see the future of communicating with teenagers not just as a teacher, but also as someone who interacts with these kids at such a pivotal time in their lives.

When I look back at my own teenage years, I would never classify myself as an angsty teen, one with a feeling of deep anxiety or dread. Sure, there were times when I can see these same emotions that I often see in the teenagers I have taught over the past twenty years; I had the same drama many teens had: the fights with friends, disappointments with boys, and conflicts with my parents, but I would have to say that I was a generally happy teen.

Luckily, I had several amazing mentors through my teens. Many of them will make an appearance through the pages of this book, and you were introduced to one already whose impact on me began with a personality clash of epic proportions.

Mentors, those trusted adults that are not the parents, can offer sound advice that your teens will actually absorb at times when they are unwilling to listen to your advice. As a parent, knowing that your teen has these other trusted adults in their life can, with your guidance, give you needed peace of mind. Teens who have benefited from impactful adult mentors are not a reflection of parental disinterest. In fact, it is important to look at which characteristics of these adult mentors parents might be able to emulate. Teens with trusted adult mentors will be strengthened by these relationships and will feel that they have someone to trust with whom they can share their burdens.

According to numerous studies, including one from the American Psychological Association (2019), there has been a dramatic change in the mental health of teens correlating to the rise of digital media. Anxiety, depression, and even suicide in teens has increased dramatically. Teens claim that the world they live in is much different than that of their parents and, to a certain extent, there is truth to this. The teens of today are growing up in a world where their entire lives are put on display. I often joke with my students that my generation was the first to send text messages. We created words out of numbers on our pagers, but this generation not only has to deal with text messaging on a whole new level, but they also contend with social media that puts their life in a spotlight. They seek attention not only from their peers in person, but also from an entire population of peers around the globe that become their mirror to the world.

As parents, your first instinct is to tell them they don't need to make these comparisons. While this is true, many teenagers simply are unable to hear this advice from you. You can still offer it, and you should, but don't be surprised when they don't take it from you. They might be able to hear it from another trusted adult or a peer, but they are at an age where they want to be an individual. All you can do is be supportive and help them to be their personal best by listening, being an example, guiding them away from the dangers, offering that unwanted advice, and being positive as often as humanly possible.

Teenagers can cause increased stress and make you question your parenting skills. They make you wonder how they could go from this sweet loving child to this new person they have become as a teenager, one who used to tell you everything and now you feel like they are keeping things from you.

The general consensus is to believe the following:

- Teens are overly dramatic and completely selfish.
- It is their hormones creating the attitude they toss around to everyone who is in their path.
- Teenagers believe that life revolves around them.
- It is a phase they are going through that everyone just has to tolerate and suffer through.

However, I believe that all this drama masks the underlying issues. If you communicate with your teen, it will drive deeper relationships and reveal the "how's" and "whys" of your teenager. Because while some of it can be explained by biology and psychology, each teen is still essentially dealing with their own stuff. They are not all alike. Wouldn't that be scary?

My favorite part of being a teacher has always been making connections with teens. Seeing them for who they are beyond the student who sits in a desk in my classroom. It is also why I became a transformational coach for parents and teens. It is one of the many reasons I am writing this book.

In this book, I am not going to tell you how to parent, but as a parent, some of what you read might make you uncomfortable. Your job is to protect your children at all costs, but what if by protecting them, you are doing more harm than good? What if by wanting to be their friend you are pushing them away? Throughout this book, there will be stories from my own personal experiences, stories that have been shared with me by others, and stories that come from secondary sources. Some of the stories will touch your heart, some of these stories may make you angry, and your emotions may be all over the place. I will ask you to think about what you already know and, in some cases, question it. I will ask you to listen with more than just your ears to pay attention to all the nuances of communication that go along with being in the life of a teenager.

I am not a parent; although, I have been asked by parents how to parent more than once during my teaching career. The first time this happened, my mouth fell open. I was barely out of school myself, and I had a parent ask me how to discipline her child. She had tried everything and didn't know what to do. She told me that she tried to ground him, but she just couldn't stick with it. It was a good thing we were on the phone at the time because I know my reaction was not very professional. I just didn't understand. Twenty years later and that conversation would have gone a lot differently. It is not my job to teach parents how to parent their children, but I can now help parents and their children communicate on a different level.

You are the parent. There is no doubt of that. Your teens wouldn't respect you if you did not show them how to be good adults, but they want you to lead by example and guide them. They *want* to be disciplined when they do wrong, but what they really want is to be heard and seen, even when they are pushing back. Because teenagers communicate with more than words, parenting teens is tough. They make it tougher, but it's definitely worth the challenge.

When I first started teaching, I had just graduated from college and was beginning my student teaching year. I was twenty-four years old and was given both sophomore and senior classes to teach. I was only six years older than the students in my senior class, and as I have come to learn, my frontal lobe was nearing its final stages of development but still maturing (more on this in chapter one).

I was also working as an assistant to the athletic trainer, until I became a certified athletic trainer. I spent many hours in the training room, which allowed me to build an additional rapport with the students.

Teenagers especially have a tough time because they are stuck in that in-between place between being a kid and so desperately wanting to be treated like an adult. Biologically, their brains are stuck there too.

As adults, we want to protect them, we want to solve their problems for them, but what these kids want is for us to listen to them, to be there for them.

As a high school English teacher, I have spent more time with my teenage students over the past twenty years than I have with my own family during the school year. Throughout this time, I have opened my classroom door beyond the hours that I teach: in the morning, at lunch, and after school. This open-door policy allows students to come talk to me about anything on their mind. Most will come talk to me about things in their life rather than classwork. They want someone to talk to who will not judge them, and who will listen, and only offer advice when asked. I have given students a place to just get away, to come, and just be, and not have to talk. Some of them want a place to blow off steam, and I have allowed them the freedom to do that whether just to yell, cry, or sometimes bang on the wall or throw their own version of a teenage tantrum without doing any physical harm to themselves, me, or the room at large. Having an outlet is important to these teens, both boys and girls.

It is impossible to listen while speaking and trying to be heard yourself. With that in mind, are you really listening? Because that's what it takes. It takes the ability to stop and listen with your whole being. Listen with your ears, with your eyes, with your heart. Above all, listen from their perspective. If you do all these things, you will be able to communicate more effectively with your teenagers and give them a fighting chance to become amazing adults.

I had a student tell me a story that is not uncommon for teens to have to deal with. This is a student who comes to talk to me often. She would talk about the fact that the relationship with her parents was strained. She didn't feel like she could talk to either her mom or her dad. Her parents were divorced, and both had remarried. She kept talking about "an incident" that occurred that had caused this rift between her and her parents. Ultimately, she revealed that she had snuck a boy into her brother's room at night when her brother wasn't home, and her parents were sleeping. They got caught kissing in her brother's room. Her parents freaked out. Now obviously discipline was in order for breaking rules, but this went further than that and her father refused to talk to her or even look at her. According to the teen, her father told her, "I don't see you as a daughter anymore. No daughter of mine would do something like that." Her mother told her that she didn't really want to talk to her and the only reason she didn't beat the crap out of her was that she herself had made out with boys when she was young. There are religious implications to the strong reactions of the parents, but the teen ultimately felt like she was being slut-shamed more than being punished for the act that she had actually committed. She was afraid to talk to her parents. Luckily, her relationship with her mother had improved somewhat, but she still felt like she was a burden on her at times. She still struggled with her relationship with her dad. She felt unloved by her dad and that she couldn't talk to him about anything. She had been suicidal at a previous point in her life and this event triggered a depression in her. Her mother put her back in therapy after they were finally able to talk again to get her some coping skills, but her father refused to believe she even needed therapy thinking she was just being dramatic. Even if these feelings are just the perception of the teen, this *was* how she felt. This resulted in a communication problem. The reactions of these parents created ripples for this child and now she is wary of trusting them.

As a teacher, but not a parent, the students come to me for advice for a plethora of reasons. Some for the sheer sake that I am an adult who has dealt with many of their kind. Some because I am someone to trust because I am not one of your kind, namely, a parent, and some just want to pick my brain and see if they will get an answer they like. I If they don't, they lump me in the general category of being an adult who doesn't know anything.

Last year, I gave my students a survey about their parents. One of the questions asked was, "what is the biggest mistake their own parents or parents in general make in regard to teenagers?" The answer that kept showing up the most often was "parents don't listen and they don't communicate." One student replied, "I believe that a lot of parents don't really listen to their teens, they just think they know them, but in reality, many teens hide things from their parents because they're afraid of judgment, disappointment, and punishment. Some teens do try talking to their guardians, but sometimes parents are distracted or just shrug them away."

As parents, guardians, coaches, teachers, or any other adult in a teenager's life, it is your job to take your communication beyond listening. To understand how to see beyond the teenage mask to develop deeper, richer, and more positive relationships with your teens.

This book will provide you with the tools you need to foster the relationships you would like to have with these teens. It will also provide you with insight directly from the mouths of teenagers. I have interviewed and given questionnaires to many of the teens I have had the pleasure to teach, and I cherish the honesty of their responses. I am sharing them with you in the hopes that you will truly see them and hear what they have to say.

One of the best ways I can help these teens is to help you, the parents, understand where they are coming from and in many cases, you will see I have asked them directly. Their responses are poignant and honest. Pay attention. I also recommend asking your own teens many of these questions. Their answers may surprise you, horrify you, or even delight you.

Open your eyes and your heart. Go beyond listening and really see, hear, and feel your teenager. That's what it will take to communicate with your teen more effectively, which is my sincerest desire.

I don't have all the answers. My goal is to show you a little bit of the background into why they act like they do and how to approach communicating with them during this time in their lives through research, my own experiences, others' stories, and from the teens themselves, as well as ways for you to process how you feel about it all.

CHAPTER 1

THE HISTORY OF TEENAGE CONFLICT: WHY IT'S VERY NORMAL

———

Best friends Jane and Molly dropped their backpacks on the dining room table as they came in Jane's house together after school, talking animatedly.

Jane's mom, Veronica, was working on her computer on the same dining room table and said, "Hey girls."

Not even stopping the flow of their conversation to look at Veronica, they offered a brief wave as they headed into the kitchen to grab drinks and snacks before settling in on the couch and clicking on the TV.

Veronica, pretending to continue to work, strained to hear what the girls were talking about. This was her favorite time of the day, as she often got to catch up on what was going on in Jane's life by eavesdropping on Jane and Molly's after-school chats.

Veronica heard Molly say to Jane, "Can you believe Griffin just punched him like that?"

Veronica stopped typing. Griffin was Jane's boyfriend. She was super curious now.

Jane replied, "Jeff has been my best guy friend since kindergarten. Griff needs to get over himself, I'm so mad at him."

"I think it's sweet that he's jealous," Molly cooed.

"You wouldn't think it was so sweet if he were your boyfriend. He doesn't want me hanging out with Jeff anymore."

Veronica closed her laptop and headed over to the couch. She sat down next to Jane and said, "Did I ever tell you about the time when your dad did the same thing when we were in high school?"

Cue the eye roll.

Because what is the likelihood that Jane was happy that her mother jumped in on this private moment? Not likely, right? Do you remember moments like this with your parents? Those OMG! Help me! My parents are embarrassing me, moments. I was one of the few who would've probably invited my mom to join in on the conversation, but it would have depended on the day, the hour, the minute (if you ask her, my mom will agree).

Conflict is a natural part of parenting teens. How you deal with that conflict will determine the type of relationship you end up having with your teen. It is natural for teenagers to begin pulling away from their parents. They are trying to figure out their role in the confusing world of not quite being a child, but not yet an adult either. I will keep repeating this concept over and over again throughout this book because understanding their confusion is very important as you try to grapple with what is happening in the mind of your teenager.

In essence, they want to have their cake and eat it too. They want you to instinctively know when they want you to treat them like an adult and when they want you to treat them like a child. I even had a student say that as adults we just know when to do this. I actually laughed out loud when I read this. Partly because of the honesty of the answer and partly because this proves one of the points I want to make in this book; communication is severely lacking between teens and adults. They expect us to be able to read their minds.

As you read below how the teenage brain works and the psychology and strategies mentioned throughout this book, I want you to think about this statement my student made. Instinctually, parents and other adults who work with teenagers can decide when to treat them like children and when to treat them like adults, but it will only be through effective communication that this will produce meaningful results.

OOOOOOOOOOOOOOOOOOOOOOOOOOOOOOOOO

In the past, people believed that the brain stopped developing prior to adolescence; however, over the past fifteen to twenty years, researchers have found that the teenage brain is much more complex than they ever imagined and continues to develop throughout adolescence not stopping until the mid-twenties.

Did you know that the same things that you might be complaining about your teenagers now Socrates and Aristotle were complaining about young people as early as 469-399 BC? Shakespeare was writing about in his works in the seventeenth century, and Rousseau was differentiating teenagers from children using these characteristics in the eighteenth century. Sarah-Jayne Blakemore in her book *Inventing Ourselves* takes time to remind us of these things, in order to promote the idea that your teenagers are not so different and to point out the importance of remembering your own wayward teenage years and the way you interacted with your own parents. I bet if you ask your own parents, they will say you acted in much the same way. Did your parent ever say to you when you were younger "I hope you have a child just like you?" That can be both good and bad. I saw a meme recently that said, "my kid is turning out just like me, well played Karma, well-played."

Characteristics such as bad manners, contempt for authority, disrespect for adults, things you see as excuses the teens in your life are coming up with, or teens just being overly dramatic, actually have a biological explanation. Teens just cannot help being the way they are.

This does not mean we just let them run around willy-nilly acting like fools and throw in the proverbial towel but knowing how the teenage brain works will give you insight, understanding, patience, and hopefully a little compassion for all that is going on inside the heads of these adolescents. You might just learn not to take the things your teenagers say and do quite so personally as well. Immaturity hurts, but remember their brains are still growing; they are not as mature as they think they are.

One of the most common questions that parents ask about their teenagers is "what happened to my sweet lovable child?" One day they were this sweet child and now they have become this emotional teenager who I don't recognize. What do I do now?

Let's take a look at why it happens in the first place.

The teenage brain develops from the back to the front. Anatomically, what this means is that the emotional centers of the brain, which are located in the limbic system, develop fully before the pre-frontal cortex—the part of the brain that is responsible for executive functions such as judgment and perspective-maintaining. Emotions are in overdrive while judgment, impulse control, and empathy have not yet fully caught up. This doesn't fully happen for many teens until their mid-twenties. A huge restructuring is happening during this period of adolescence. Think of it like a massive upgrade to the brain's network and wiring. When it is finished it will be a well-oiled machine, but the process is time-consuming and while the process is in progress, it feels a bit clunky.

What does this mean? Different parts of the brain develop at different rates. What this tells us is there is a disconnect between the way teenagers react in certain situations.

Don't mistake this explanation for me saying that teenagers should not be held responsible for their actions. I am not saying this at all nor am I saying that the adults in their lives should not continue to teach them right from wrong. The point here is to give you an understanding of why your seemingly normal child, and their dear friends, seem to have lost their ever-loving minds. The teenage wiring is off balance. So, your teenager is more immature in an area that can heighten his or her sense of anxiety, depression, and other emotions that make your teen seem unstable.

Do you see the problem? There is a disconnect between the overactive emotional centered limbic system and the underdeveloped rational problem-solving, decision-making frontal lobe. The best example I can give is that this is like having a Ferrari engine with golf cart brakes. The brakes won't hold. The emotions will win out again and again.

The plasticity of their brains will allow your teen to recover from a lot of this. Neuroplasticity is the ability of the brain to form new connections, pathways, and change how its circuits are wired. The child and the teenage brain have the capacity to change more than at any time in life. In *The Teenage Brain*, Frances Jensen lets us know which processes are affected. "Thinking, planning, learning, acting—all influence the brain's physical structure and functional organization, according to the theory of neuroplasticity." She also says that the following attributes are seen during this time period:

1. Memories are easier to make and last longer during the teen years than the adult years
2. Time to identify strengths and focus on emerging talents
3. Get the best results from remediation and special help for learning and emotional issues.

So, there is hope. Your teen will bounce back, but your support is needed in the meantime.

〇〇〇〇〇〇〇〇〇〇〇〇〇〇〇〇〇〇〇〇〇〇〇〇〇〇〇

In 2011, David Dobbs published an article in *National Geographic* entitled "Beautiful Brains," in which he tells a story about his son who had phoned him to tell him he had gotten in trouble for driving a "little fast" on the highway. Think of a number you believe this teenager would think of as a "little fast." Eighty? Eighty-five? Ninety? How about 113? Yep. His son had been driving 113 miles per hour on the highway.

Now his son was actually "somber and contrite" as Dobbs describes it. He did not object to his punishments, and he did not argue when Dobbs explained that "if anything happens at that speed—a dog in the road, a blown tire, a sneeze—he dies." Dobbs explains that his son was in fact "irritatingly reasonable" about all of this. His son even admitted that the cop was right to pull him over. But his son had one objection to the whole thing; one of the citations he received was for "reckless driving." What was your reaction to this objection just then? Did you roll your eyes? Did you think "that figures"? Does it surprise you or the opposite, not surprise you in the least?

Actually, your reaction is not the point at all. The point is to pay attention to Dobbs's son's perception of the word reckless and his response when Dobbs asks him "What would you call it?"

Here is his son's response, and while you are reading it, I want you to think about why this response is so important in the discussion of the teenage brain.

His son responded very calmly that reckless was not accurate. "Reckless sounds like you're not paying attention. But I was. I made a deliberate point of doing this on an empty stretch of dry interstate, in broad daylight, with good sight lines and no traffic. I mean, I wasn't just gunning the thing. I was driving."

David Dobbs describes this same scenario in a more positive light his interview on NPR with B. J. Casey and Dr. Jay Giedd. He says it was not as simple as his just being an idiot. In fact, "it was a more positive agenda. He was going after something instead of just lacking something."

Dr. Kenneth Ginsburg discusses this risk phenomenon in a different way in his interview with Kristen and Liz on their *Spawned Parenting* podcast. He believes teenagers are super learners rather than inherent risk takers. "Teenagers are not risk takers. They are natural experimenters, they're going to always test their limits, they are going to always expand their horizons, they're always going to go to the edge of existing knowledge." It becomes important to create "golden opportunities at those edges, really enriching opportunities where they can have thrills in school, on the sports field, in communication, in theater," so these teenagers feel fulfilled. Ginsburg also states, "when it becomes a risk is when they don't have the clear, stop measures."

This means your teens need boundaries. They, in fact, crave them. But Ginsburg makes it clear that these boundaries should keep your teen safe, "but what you're never going to do, and what you would never want to do is to shut down experimentation, not if you want a smart thirty-five-year-old, not if you want a smart fifty-year-old, because now is the time they're cramming that knowledge in. We want them to have every experience they can."

Because of the disconnect during this period in their lives, teens place much more emphasis on reward, because of that overactive limbic system, which is why peer acceptance is so important to them. They have become more self-aware as well, meaning that they are coming into their own. They see themselves as an individual and rely less on their family to make decisions for and with them. They have a great need to make their own choices.

They are less reasoned in their decision-making. The consequences of their behavior affect teens differently; they are less sensitive to negative consequences and more sensitive to rewards. Because they have a harder time engaging their frontal lobe, they have a harder time resisting temptation. Frances Jensen explains in *The Teenage Brain*, "it is not the perception of the risk, but the anticipation of the reward despite the risk."

Here's a great example of this: one day the school nurse came running across the hall to my classroom asking for my help. This was not unusual, as I am an athletic trainer, so she often came to have me look at injured students; however, the student we were looking at that day had done something very unusual. On a five-dollar dare, he had snorted ghost pepper sauce! Some of you might have gasped. If you did not, that means you are unaware of what a ghost pepper is. A ghost pepper is one of the hottest peppers in the world. So, for five dollars this kid had put ghost pepper sauce in his sinus cavity! Needless to say, his face was swollen, and he was in a lot of pain. The nurse had no idea what to do. I had a student go get milk from the cafeteria, and we flushed his sinuses with the milk and then flushed them several times with saline water to remove the milk. It worked. When the student was out of pain, we asked the million-dollar question, "why on earth would you do something like that?" His teenage brain responded "I would do anything for money." That reward center sensitivity at its finest. The five dollars was worth more to him than the pain in his sinus cavity.

Teenagers are also not as efficient or quick in making decisions. Hence the last-minute trips to Michael's for that trifold board that every student seems to need for their science project they knew about three weeks ago but is due the next day. This is where parents need to be proactive and communicate with their teens by possibly asking on Sunday night, "what does your week and weekend look like this week? Any tests, projects due, etc." So, they know when they have to Uber their kids around ahead of time and can put cash aside for the added expenses. They may still not remember about the project because it is not a high priority, but you can mitigate some of the fallout by the attempt.

Teenagers have heightened emotions on all levels without the developed ability for impulse control, judgment, and empathy. This goes a long way to explain the teenage outbursts and the end-of-the-world feeling about everything happening in their life. They also do not have the life experience to balance their feelings.

This is not an excuse for their behavior; however, it grants an explanation for why it occurs. As adults, this information should then assist us in becoming empathetic and understanding, rather than standing in judgment or becoming frustrated with the teens in our circle.

Some researchers believe that there is an evolutionary reason behind why teenagers act the way that they do, and it puts their actions in a more positive light using natural selection as its foundation. David Dobbs in the *National Geographic* article "Beautiful Brains" sums it up in the following. "Selection is hell on dysfunctional traits. If adolescence is essentially a collection of them—angst, idiocy, and haste impulsiveness, selfishness, and reckless bumbling—then how did those traits survive selection? They couldn't—not if they were the period's most fundamental or consequential features."

There are four broad categories at the heart of this theory: excitement, novelty, risk and the company of peers. While teenagers find much trouble in these areas, they can also lead to positive interactions that actually help them as they become adults.

For example, Dobbs says that "the urge to meet more people... can create a wider circle of friends, which generally makes us happier, safer, and more successful."

In terms of risk, the age group comprised of fourteen-to-seventeen-year-olds is the biggest group of risk-takers, but it is not because they do not think about the risk. My student who snorted the ghost pepper sauce is a prime example. Or how about this one, one day I was teaching and all of a sudden one of my seniors screams "Ow!" I look over and he is holding one of my staplers open, you know, like when you would hang something on the wall, and also holding his leg.

> Me: What happened?
> Student: The staple went into my leg.
> Me: (giving him my teacher look)
> Student: What? I didn't think it would go through flesh.
> Whole class: (laughter)
> Me: (shaking my head)

You know I can't make this stuff up.

In fact, studies have shown that teens overestimate the risk; however, they value the reward more than adults. David Dobbs also discusses in "Beautiful Brains" the views of researchers Lawrence Steinberg and B. J. Casey, whose work shows this risk versus reward has been part of our evolutionary selection process because it gives us an "adaptive edge" in the ability to learn the skills necessary to "get out of the house and into new turf" and to leave the safety of home and move out into the scary real world.

B. J. Casey further discusses this idea in the same interview on NPR with David Dobbs and Jay Giedd. She agrees with the idea that the prefrontal cortex, our logic center, doesn't function the same way in adolescents as it does in adults. She states that

> "deep structures in the brain that are involved in desire
> and our emotions, those systems seem to be really
> pulling and maturing at a time in adolescence that
> really allow the individual to leave the home. If our
> children weren't experimenting, if they weren't telling

us about their bad behavior and the sort, we may be more inclined to want to keep them in the home."

Casey gets a laugh at this point in the interview because every parent knows how it feels when their teen has done something to make them wonder how much longer they are going to be living under their roof. This bad behavior, however, not only allows the parents to let go of the reins but it also allows for learning to occur on the part of the teen. Casey leads to the question of "why the brain would be made this way to put teenagers in harm's way?" Ultimately, the point Casey is making is that the teenage brain is helping prepare the teenager for independent living as an adult.

oooooooooooooooooooooooooooooo

Teens prefer the company of their peers more than the company of adults, but this is for more positive reasons. According to this more naturally selective theory discussed by Casey, Dobbs, and Giedd, this can be for novelty and "to invest in the future rather than the past." As we grow up, we spend the first part of our lives with our parents, but we spend the biggest part of our lives, adulthood, "and prosper (or not) in a world run and remade by our peers. Knowing, understanding, and building relationships with them bears critically on success." However, this also explains why peer exclusion is such a dramatic thing for teenagers. In "Beautiful Brains," Dobbs discusses that some brain scans show, "our brains react to peer exclusion much as they respond to threats to physical health or food supply." Add that to the emotionally reactive teenage brain, and it becomes much easier to comprehend why a thirteen-year-old gets hysterical when deceived by a friend, or a fifteen-year-old becomes depressed at not being invited to a party. Daniel Siegel, author of *Brainstorm*, rightly states, "if adults try to block the flow of adolescence, it is likely that communication, so important to relationships, will be tainted with tension and disrespect."

Teenagers are also influenced by their peers through what is deemed the imaginary audience. The imaginary audience is based around the perceived audience reacting to you at any given time. According to David Elkind, it is at the point of adolescence, at around age eleven or twelve, that a child can truly discern the thoughts of others. This new ability poses a problem because while the adolescent becomes aware of the thoughts of others he is "unable to differentiate between what others are thinking about and his own mental preoccupations, he assumes that other people are as obsessed with his behavior and appearance as he is himself." Drew Cingel is moving Elkind's research into the social media age. Cingel finds that the obsession that teenagers have with this imaginary audience is directly linked to their social media use. Cingel tells Maiken Scott on his podcast *The Pulse*, "the more kids used social media the more they thought about their imaginary audience." In this same podcast, a senior, Amanda, is used as an example. Amanda imagines her friends, family members, strangers—they are all looking at her pictures and judging her. "How many likes I get on this picture would determine if I'm pretty or not, and like 'whoa, I'm popular because I have 200 likes.'" This is the reality for so many teens. They post pictures to boost their self-esteem. To validate their beauty.

Teenagers focus on the present. Everything about their lives is immediate. They are not thinking about what happens in the future like you might be. For example, asking some teenagers "what do you want to do with the rest of your life?" might actually cause them to panic. They may have some glimmer of an idea, but for some of them this is too far in the future and some smaller goal would be more motivational.

The one thing a teenager does *not* want to hear is that their feelings at the moment are insignificant. For example, the age-old saying that I'm sure you heard when we were growing up in some form just like I did, "don't worry there are plenty of other fish in the sea." I know I didn't want to hear it when I was that age, did you? It definitely does not matter to them that the overwhelming feelings they are experiencing at the moment will go away. It only matters that these feelings are happening right at the moment. The instant you devalue or make light of their feelings you lose them, especially if anyone else is around.

The same is true for trying to solve the problem if they don't want your help. As you will see later in this book through many examples from teenagers I have interacted with, what they really want is for you to listen and be honest with them. They want you to pay attention and communicate with them in a way that shows that you are truly engaging and that you are trying to understand the problem from their perspective.

Celebrate the differences in their brain wiring. Understand where they are coming from. It will make your job as a parent much easier.

CHAPTER 2

DIFFERENCES BETWEEN THEN AND NOW

———

"Ms. Jass, did you hear that Johnny got suspended today for looking at porn on a school computer?"

My eyes bugged out of my head and my mouth dropped open. "He's only in eighth grade," ran through my head.

I proceed to open the tab in my grading program to verify this shocking information. The tab opened:

"Suspended for five days for looking at inappropriate content on a school device."

I'd like to think of myself as pretty well-informed when it comes to what goes on in classrooms these days, but a couple of years ago, I taught seventh and eighth grade for the first time. I realized there is a big difference between the tweens and the teenagers I am so familiar with. Parents of tweens, you are either laughing at me or shaking your head at my naivety. In retrospect, I shouldn't have been as shocked as I was. If you are just as shocked as I am, here is a staggering fact. Cara Natterson in her book *Decoding Boys* points out that half of all eleven-year-old boys have viewed porn and, "researchers clearly agree that by the end of middle school the majority of boys have been porn exposed."

I do remember my brother and cousin finding my uncle's *Playboy* magazines during those same tween years, and my friends watching porn on pirated cable channels in high school.

This idea that something like porn is so readily available is something parents need to be aware of, and it is one of those things that is different than it was back when we were kids. It's literally at their fingertips.

Do you remember when you were a teenager and you said to your parents "it's different now than when you were a teenager"? If you didn't say it, I'm sure you thought it. I know the thought crossed my mind a time or two.

Recently, I had a conversation with my mom and my sister-in-law's mom about this exact topic. They began sharing about staying out playing until the streetlights came on. I said, "we did that too." We knew to come in either when the streetlights came on, or it got dark, or my mom stood on the porch and whistled for us to come in.

Both of them shared other things that I was able to say, "we did that too." The differences in our childhoods had more to do with where we grew up and occasionally with how much our parents were able to provide us with, but the "differences" in our childhoods were not that much different. My mom was born in the 1940s, my sister-in-law's mom was born in the '60s, and I was born in the '70s.

I put a post on Facebook asking, "when you were a teenager and you said 'things were different when you were my age' to your parents, what were you talking about and in what decade were you a teen?" One of my FB friends replied, "It is so so very different today. The '80s were a breeze to be a teen compared to now."

Another one was more concerned with economics. She said, "this is probably going to sound weird, but I remember my senior year '95. I told my mom that I was going to have to work until I died because social security would be bankrupt. She asked what I was talking about, and I told her my economics teacher had said her generation would be the last one to get social security. She said that was crap, but I remember crying uncontrollably and saying I'm never going to have the life you guys have. I'll be poor forever."

Yet another friend was also a teen in the '90s; she said "when I said this to my parent, I think it was just me saying that there's just no way they could understand what I was going through. My parents were both pretty sheltered and from religious families. Now that I'm older, I understand that they can relate in some ways. It took me until my mid-thirties to start seeing my parents as real people (lol emoji) and not 'just my parents.'"

But when Gen Z says, "it's different now than when you were a teenager," there really is something to it. They are the first generation to have grown up with the internet demanding their attention for almost their entire lives. It impacts them the most as soon as they are given access to the internet and especially social media. Think about it; when we were that age, and we were bullied at school, the bullying was limited to word of mouth. Nowadays, that bullying has unlimited reach and has the potential to do unlimited damage; their bullying literally goes viral.

According to Jonathan Haidt, PhD in the documentary *The Social Dilemma,*

> "there has been a gigantic increase in depression and anxiety for American teenagers which began right around between 2011 and 2013. The number of teenage girls out of 100,000 in this country who are admitted to a hospital every year because they cut or otherwise harm themselves, that number was pretty stable until around 2010 to 2011. And then it begins going way up. It's up 62 percent for older teen girls. It's up 189 percent for the preteen girls. That's nearly triple. Even more horrifying, we see the same pattern with suicide. The older teen girls fifteen to nineteen years old, they're up 70 percent compared to the first decade of the century, the preteen girls who have very low rates to begin with, they are up 151 percent. Gen Z, the kids born after 1996 or so, those kids are the first generation in history that got on social media in middle school."

Haidt continues to explain the phenomenon for this generation,

> "how do they spend their time? They come home from school, and they're on their devices. A whole generation is more anxious, more fragile, more depressed. They're much less comfortable taking risks. The rates at which they get driver's licenses have been dropping. The number who has ever gone out on a date or have had any kind of romantic interaction is dropping rapidly. This is a real change in a generation. And remember, for every one of these, for every hospital admission, there's a family that is traumatized and horrified."

According to a 2019 Pew Research Center study, anxiety and depression (70 percent) tops the list of problems that teens see among the peers with bullying (55 percent) and drug addiction (51 percent) also being major problems.

Teenagers today will still complain to us adults about not understanding the same things we complained about at their age: boys, school, parents, etc. My students have admitted that they believe school is harder, that life is harder, but at the heart of what makes this generation different is the ease of access to the internet and social media; it is literally in the palm of their hands.

Many of you will want answers about social media use. I don't have them. Prior to 2018, the American Academy of Child and Adolescent Psychiatry (AACAP) recommended no more than two hours of screen time for teenagers, but they have since adjusted this, and now offer different guidelines. First let me give you some statistics from Pew Research Studies done on teens and their social media habits in 2015 and 2018:

- 95 percent of teens have their own mobile devices with internet capabilities
- approximately 90 percent of teens ages thirteen to seventeen have used social media
- 75 percent report having at least one active social media profile
- 45 percent of teens say they use the internet "almost constantly"
  - Another 44 percent say they go online several times a day
    - meaning roughly nine-in-ten teens go online at least multiple times per day

- 90 percent of teens say they play video games of any kind (whether on a computer, game console or cellphone)
  - 83 percent of girls and 97 percent of boys

How much time are you on your own devices? Are you a "constant" user like most of the teens? If so, you might set an example for your own teen and put your phone away a little more often.

The AACAP no longer gives a recommended time for teens in regard to social media. Instead, they provide information sheets that recommend ways in which you can limit the amount of screen time and give ways to protect your child such as monitoring social media, adjusting privacy and location settings, teaching them not to give out private information, and knowing which apps are available to limit access to age-appropriate sites.

The reality is that you need to educate your teens and decide what is appropriate for your individual child.

As hard as parents try to monitor their kids' social media, this generation seems to find their way onto social media even if they seem to have little to no access to the internet.

Just the other day, I counseled a student whose girlfriend was posting pictures of herself in a towel on Instagram. Her parents do not allow her to have access to social media. Yet, she has been posting these pictures anyway. She is not one of the students at my school, or I might have been able to intervene more directly. But luckily her boyfriend came to me for advice because they got into a fight about it. It gave me the opportunity to give him a mini lesson on how the mind of a teenage girl works. The fight happened because he was demanding she not post the pictures. She told him when people responded to the pictures, it made her feel beautiful.

I encouraged him to let her know he preferred she didn't post the pictures, how it made him feel, and to remind her how beautiful she was. She said she wouldn't post them anymore. Unfortunately, she said she would do it for him, not for herself, but at least she won't be posting these types of pictures anymore.

While I believe there should be some trust between teens and their parents, the trust should be earned, as proven by the story above. Make sure you are aware of what is on your teen's phone. Make sure you or someone you trust is monitoring their social media activity.

Back when my cousin was a teenager and became active on social media, she is twenty-three years younger than me, there were several of us cousins who were also friends with her on her social media accounts. We were able to gently monitor what was happening, and if we became concerned, we discussed it with her and, if necessary, reported it to our uncle.

The most important thing parents, and any other adult involved in these children's lives, can do is educate them about the potential dangers. This is not limited to predators.

The documentary *The Social Dilemma* explains what social media has become, not just for teens, but for society as a whole. Tristan Harris explains that social media is not a tool because

"If something is a tool it genuinely is just sitting there waiting patiently. If something is not a tool, it's demanding things from you. It's seducing you. It's manipulating you. It wants things from you. And we've moved away from having a tools-based technology environment to an addiction and manipulation-based technology environment. That's what's changed. Social media isn't a tool that's just waiting to be used. It has its own goals, and it has its own means of pursuing them by using your psychology against you."

When applied to teenagers, this is even more frightening because their psychology is easily manipulated, especially when it comes to social media. They are seduced by the allure of connecting with others. Harris later goes on to comment that social media in particular "takes over a kid's sense of self-worth and identity" as our teenagers seek out a need for social approval.

Chamath Palihapitiya also adds to this idea of social approval in *The Social Dilemma*. He says,

"we curate our lives around this perceived sense of perfection because we get rewarded in these short-term signals: hearts, likes, thumbs up, and we conflate that with value, and we inflate it with truth. And instead, what it really is is fake brittle popularity, that's short term and that leaves you even more vacant and empty than before you did it. Because then it forces you into this vicious cycle where you're like, what's the next thing I need to do now because I need to get it back. Think about that compounded by two billion people, and then think about how people react based on the perceptions of others. It's just... it's really bad. It's really, really bad."

Like the others, Palihapitiya is talking about all of us, but when forced to look at this through the perspective of the teenager and coupled with Dr. Haidt's statistics, it's really frightening.

According to one of my students, it is important to "listen to what teenagers have to say before you can say anything. Unlike the '60s, '70s, '80s, etc., the world is completely different right now. Gen Z develops as technology does, often leading to various emotions such as stress, depression, and anxiety that comes from school, relationships, and social media. Just hearing them out can help parents understand a teenager's situation."

So, when we think back to our saying things were different when we were teenagers from when our parents were teenagers, to the current teenagers saying it to us now, we really need to take a step back before making the old retort, "I remember what it was like being a teenager, it wasn't that different." Because can you really say it wasn't?

Even if what they are talking about is school, grades, relationships, or something that you think you can relate to, remember the other pressures they are dealing with. Many of their lives are being lived in a world that is under a macroscope, a viral world that everyone can see.

Try to take a beat and see it from their perspective. Remember that you thought everything was larger than life when you were their age and remember that things really are on a much bigger platform now. Be honest with yourself, be honest with your teen, and work from that place of honesty to build your relationship. Having a healthy dose of empathy won't hurt either.

And while social media and technology are subjects parents are eager to delve into because of their prevalence, this is just one of the many facets of your teen's life. Having the same concern and interest in other areas of their life is equally as important as we will continue to explore throughout this book.

What You Can Do as a Parent?

- Educate your teen about the dangers of social media—repeatedly. They need to hear it over and over again even if you annoy them.
- Monitor your teen's social media—either yourself or have a trusted friend or family member help you do it.
- Set an example for your teen with social media use and amount of screen time.
- Don't say "when I was your age." Feel free to share stories about your past but not to compare.
- Remember it's all vital to them now—don't minimize their feelings.

CHAPTER 3

POSITIVE VS. NEGATIVE REINFORCEMENT

———

When we were kids, my brother and I had a habit of not listening to my mother when she yelled. She would stand at the bottom of the stairs yelling up at my brother and me, who were at the top of the stairs. My brother and I would look at each other and laugh. This would continue until she yelled the dreaded words, "wait until your father gets home." At which point, Jason and I would sit down on the stairs and stop laughing and share a look of dread and the question "what will dad do when he gets home?" in both of our eyes.

Mom still denies saying "wait till dad gets home." Even better yet, nothing would happen when "dad got home" except he would give us that horrifying look of disappointment, which was more potent than the yelling, and according to my mom, when she recounted to him what had happened, he also would remind her "who is the child?"

One year for Mother's Day, we even bought my mother a gag gift from Spencer's Gifts. It was a little speaker box that said things when you pushed its buttons. We bought it because it sounded exactly like my mom. It said things like, "You're gonna poke your eye out with that thing," "Stop it," "The answer is no," and "It's broken, are you happy now?" We still have it somewhere.

ᴓᴓᴓᴓᴓᴓᴓᴓᴓᴓᴓᴓᴓᴓᴓᴓᴓᴓᴓᴓᴓᴓᴓᴓᴓᴓᴓᴓ

When I first started teaching, I tended to be a yeller. One year, I was even voted in the teacher superlatives for the yearbook "Most Likely to Throw a Fit." It was a fun picture to take.

"Today, we are going to be finishing the assignment we started yesterday," I announced to my tenth graders, "please take out the documents we were working with yesterday."

The students followed my directions. All except Greg, who had recently been moved near the front of the room because he had been caught repeatedly using his phone. I walked calmly over to Greg's desk and whispered to him to take out his materials. Then I headed back up to the front of the room and turned around.

Greg hadn't moved.

"Please take out your materials" I said, my voice slightly elevated. Greg crossed his arms and slumped into his desk.

"Greg, take out your materials *now!*"

"Why are you yelling at me?"

When I first started teaching, I never had trouble with classroom management even though I was only six to eight years older than the students I was teaching. Depending on who asked, I had several answers for why this was. One response was, "I was raised by coaches." During my own high school years, I spent my time after school in the training room and on the athletic fields with coaches who had loud booming voices who commanded the attention of their athletes with both the volume and the inspiration of their words. Coaches like Coach Takk, who I mentioned in my introduction, and Coach John Link, both of whom had a tremendous impact on me during my teenage years as both high school mentors, colleagues, and friends. Both men had big personalities and commanded respect without demanding it. They expected you to be your best self.

Another answer I would give is that I have my mother's voice and my father's look. My mother was the one who yelled in our house. You would've thought I would've learned faster that yelling was not the way to go in my classroom. You see, it didn't work well with my brother and me. Apparently, that look of disappointment is much more productive than any amount of yelling I could ever do in the classroom.

My students over the years would continue to ask me "why are you yelling at me?" As a young teacher, I would think they were ridiculous. What do you mean why was I yelling at them? They were obviously doing something wrong, or I wouldn't be yelling at them in the first place. Right?

As the years went on, and I matured as a teacher, I yelled less and paid more attention to what was going on around me. This didn't mean I didn't fall into the bad old habit of yelling. Old habits do die hard, but I became aware of what the yelling meant to them.

It wasn't that they didn't recognize they were doing something wrong. Most of the time when cooler heads prevailed on both sides, the student could identify the behavior that had triggered my yelling, but they also identified the fact that yelling did not solve the problem. Oftentimes they would say something like, "I get yelled at enough at home" or "I shouldn't have to be yelled at during school too."

While there are some teenagers who feed off of negative attention, this is generally because they have had so much negativity in their lives that they don't know what to do with positive feedback.

What can happen at home is that parents focus too heavily on negative behaviors, and teens respond only to the negativity. Your children, especially your teens, then come to expect and need that negative attention from you and act out to get it. This can be both conscious and subconscious behavior.

One of the best ways to teach positive behavior is to model that behavior yourself. You thought your children were watching you when they were little, but they have only become more observant the older they have become. As was discussed in chapter one, these teenagers are learning how to become adults, and they are watching the closest adults in their lives to learn how to do this. What you do matters and more than ever now that they will be mimicking your behaviors on how to act in the "real world."

They will emulate you in how to act in a relationship, how to treat other people, your work ethic, etc. Your actions, your words, your mannerisms, they all impact your teenagers. How you treat them, and others, matters.

ᴑᴑᴑᴑᴑᴑᴑᴑᴑᴑᴑᴑᴑᴑᴑᴑᴑᴑᴑᴑᴑᴑᴑᴑᴑᴑᴑᴑᴑᴑᴑᴑᴑᴑ

One day in class last year, I asked my sophomore students the following question, "how and by whom should children be taught appropriate behavior?" The answer for "by whom" was what you would expect. Most of them said their parents. However, "the how" answers made me sad.

I was expecting the students to give me an example that showed positive reinforcement. Even through all that I had seen and heard through my career, I never expected that I would have to prompt the students for the answer that seemed so obvious to me.

Maybe, as you are reading this, you are thinking the same answer I will give you in just a minute, but first I'm going to give you the answer that the majority of the students in all five of my classes gave to me, and at this time I was teaching both sophomores and seniors. They said the way that children should be taught appropriate behavior was through punishment. I realized at that moment that this is how most of our teenagers view the world. They expect to be punished for their actions. They do not expect praise.

So, we had a discussion about the words that they had just said, and as an English teacher whose life is words, I broke down the way those words didn't make sense together. I told them that they were not wrong for their thoughts because that is their perspective, and I want them to see this clearly. Their perspective is everything and will be talked about over and over again in this book. But this was clearly a teachable moment for me. We talked about the fact that I asked about appropriate behavior and we defined appropriate. This was positive behavior. Then I asked them how they thought positive behavior should be taught.

Eventually, one or two of the students got where I was going with this and said through adults setting a good example. So, we went back to the original question of how appropriate behavior *should* be taught. Yes, I emphasized the should because obviously in these teenage minds, punishment was how many of them thought they were receiving their examples of appropriate behavior.

This year I asked my senior students how children should be taught appropriate behavior. I received many of the same answers, but I also received some more encouraging answers as well. I wanted to share with you some of the answers that show that your teens understand and see the effect of being raised both with good strong examples and recognize that not all parents do it that way:

- "By seeing healthy relationships with their parents, they can reflect that with their personal relationships with others."
- "Children should be taught appropriate behavior through their parents. I truly believe that everything starts from home, and that parents should be a child's role model. Parents should instill morals, values, and discipline in their children. Parents should also teach their children to always have manners and be respectful to others."
- "Children should be taught appropriate behavior by learning to be respectful and the right and wrong things to do."
- "They should be taught manners by parents, siblings, friends showing appropriate behavior in front of them so they can learn and have great behavior."
- "I believe that children should be demonstrated the appropriate behavior then explained why it's appropriate."
- "Children should be taught appropriate behavior by showing them from right and wrong, and also be disciplined when doing the wrong behavior so that way they learn not to do those things over again."
- "I believe that it is common sense to learn the difference between yes and no. You have to reward good behavior and find a replacement for bad behavior."

- "I think they should encourage their children and give them a lot of affection. Praise their good behavior and reward them."
- "Through communication, I believe that communication is key when it comes to teaching children right and wrong."

One teenager admits, "children should be taught appropriate behavior by their parents teaching them their life experiences." They really do want to know about your life. They may roll their eyes. They may say, "but it's not the same", as I talked about in the previous chapter. They may get embarrassed by some of the things you share, but they still want to hear it. It is a connection being made, and they crave that connection. They also want to and can learn from your mistakes.

A student of mine suggests, "maybe children should be taught appropriate behavior by putting them in situations and when they do something wrong you guide them to what's right." This was also suggested by Josh Shipp in his book *The Grown-Up's Guide to Teenage Humans*. The idea of rehearsing with your teens the various things that might go wrong and letting them come up with the answers so that they have contingency plans when things don't turn out as planned. For example, what if your teen leaves the house without her wallet and needs gas for her car, what would she do? What if you can't bring her money? Her phone has died? And her charging cord is on her bed at home? This type of role-playing is also done in the workforce to show employees how to handle on-the-job situations, especially in customer service-based companies, so this is a real-life training skill as well.

One senior believes "children should be taught behaviors through examples and situations, with trial and error. If they do commit a mistake, there should be an environment where they can try once more and learn from that same experience. Start from less pressured environments for children, such as ordering food from restaurants, or running some minor errands anyone should be capable of doing. But this comes from personal experience, and according to my parents, it was a success." Instead of looking at this as trial and error like this student does, think of in terms like Brooklyn Raney does in her book *One Trusted Adult*. Teens need us to begin letting go of the reins. They need us less than we think they do and by allowing them to do things like my student mentions, such as ordering food from restaurants or running minor errands on their own, we are giving them their own voice and training them to become "self-sufficient, functioning, and responsible adult[s]."

Or there is the much simpler action of letting your teen know that you have their back no matter what. If they are out with friends and something happens, you will come pick them up any time, day or night, without overreacting. That doesn't mean they won't receive some form of discipline if necessary. Positivity does not preclude discipline, but positivity is necessary to build communication with your teen.

Jon Gordon teaches this lesson in his book *Positive Dog.* "We all have two dogs inside of us. One dog is positive, happy, optimistic, and hopeful. The other dog is negative, mad, sad, pessimistic, and fearful. These two dogs often fight inside us, but guess who wins the fight? The one you feed the most." It is so important not only to teach your teens to feed their own positive dog but to also feed it for them.

In our interview, I also asked Jon Gordon why he believed that positivity is so important for young people today. He talked about the stress and anxiety that so many kids are dealing with and that they are being bombarded with so much negativity. He also says, "adults have a lot of issues with mental health. Can you imagine what kids are dealing with? They're not even equipped to have the experience to learn how to deal with it." He thinks, "now more than ever kids need to learn how to build resilience and grit and optimism, and positivity are a big part of grit. You need to keep moving forward."

When I ask my students to list negative attributes about themselves, they find this task to be an easy one. When I ask them to list positive attributes about themselves, they have a much harder time. Some of them get really uncomfortable. One of my students wants parents to, "encourage children and give them lots of affection and also give them rewards for doing something good." They are starved for it. They hear so much negativity in their world. They are used to getting negative feedback, but many of them would have a hard time coming up with examples off the top of their head of times they had been praised for anything that wasn't monumental.

You should know, your teens do recognize the ways in which parents can be positive role models and have their own ideas on how that can be accomplished both from a young age and as they grow into their adolescent years. One student provided this example, "if you read a book to a child every night before bed, they're going to have that drive in their minds telling them that they want to do that in their own time not only at night. So as soon as you know it, they're reading daily due to one simple action by an adult."

Jon Gordon had these suggestions for parents based on his own experience as a parent of his own two teenage children.

One thing I learned, don't put pressure and stress on them… I think they have enough pressure and stress, so don't put it on them. Let them find their own way, let them find their voice, let them own what they want to do. Guide them by asking questions but let them feel autonomous in terms of what they're deciding they want to do… help them create ownership. I think a lot of times we're always telling them what to do and taking them here and you're gonna do this practice, do this lesson… and a lot of times they feel like it's your thing, not their thing. So, I would say something we've learned is not to push them so much and not put pressure on them.

Teens want responsibility, but they also recognize that they will make mistakes. They don't want to be punished and have their own ideas about what should happen when they are given responsibilities and then make those mistakes. One of my students came up with this idea: "when they fail to meet a certain standard, physical force is not required. Simply saying that they disappointed you after not holding up to a task will do the job. Giving praise is the most important part and can't be a left-out factor."

OOOOOOOOOOOOOOOOOOOOOOOOOOOOO

Boundaries are a key component in this effort to create positive reinforcement and try to limit or eliminate negative reinforcement. Even a switch from the word punishment to the word discipline can be key. In looking at the surveys my students completed for me, most of them chose the word discipline over the word punishment. Those that chose the word punishment had a much more negative mindset about their relationship with their parents. They used other negatively charged words to discuss what good parenting should entail such as kindness vs. abuse and forced vs. guided.

Here are some examples of student responses about boundaries and discipline:

- "Children should be disciplined to understand rights from wrongs but still understand that it is okay to mess up and make mistakes and learn from their mistakes and experiences."
- "Be taught that every action they make in their lives has consequences and should do the right thing even if they don't like it."
- "It never hurts to have discipline or be a little strict. Having them be spoiled all the time can change the way they act in the future by being relatively lazy and wanting things to go their way."
- "Their parents should be assertive in what is being directed, children get a sense of entitlement if you treat them as equals from an early age, so it is important to be clear that the parent is in charge but is also fairly lenient."
- "I think children should be taught appropriate behavior by discipline but not too much discipline to where the child would have resentment for the way their parents disciplined them while growing up."

Dr. Kenneth Ginsburg talked about the difference between the words punishment and discipline on the *Spawned Parenting* Podcast. He said discipline "means to teach or to guide, ideally in a loving way; it doesn't mean to control." Punishment is about control. Discipline is about setting boundaries. Ginsburg explained,

But when you set boundaries, they have to understand where the boundaries come from, and they come because you care, because you love, because you want to protect them, because you want to keep them safe, and those boundaries are not rigid, as you are able to expand your horizons, as you are able to handle more, those boundaries will also expand. My job is to monitor you and to be in communication with you, in partnership to figure out what you can handle at any given time. But there are some things that are not under negotiation, because they will never be safe in any circumstance, so I will never find acceptable your driving and drinking or driving and texting... There are certain absolutes... When your children were little, you didn't let them put their hands on the stove, but you did let them knock over a sack of flour, because you needed them to learn from experience, not to knock over the sack of flour, but you could never let them put their hand on their stove, right? Adolescence, it's the exact same thing, they're hand on the stove issues, and then there were sack of flour issues. We want them to learn from mistakes and we want to guide them."

Ginsburg's use of boundaries here is extremely important. His analogy of hands on the stove issues and sack of flour issues puts these into negotiable and non-negotiable categories for you to think about when creating boundaries with your teen child. I would recommend starting this as early as possible, so if you are reading this and you have younger children, this goes for them as well. When negotiating boundaries, the non-negotiables are the things that are detrimental to their safety. The negotiables are the things that they can learn from (no matter that it might hurt your heart at times). Learning from mistakes is necessary, without catastrophic consequences.

What You Can Do as a Parent?

- Be a positive role model to your child—they see everything.
- Be sure the positive reinforcement outweighs the negative reinforcement.
- Use discipline (guidance) vs. punishment (control).
- Set boundaries defined by negotiables and non-negotiables.

CHAPTER 4

LISTENING BEYOND WORDS

Sixteen-year-old Erin looked at her phone. The last text from Jennifer read: "Why aren't you talking to me?"

Her stomach was in knots. She hadn't talked to Jennifer since school got out on Friday. She really needed advice, but this time she couldn't turn to her best friend since it was her best friend that was the problem. She really couldn't turn to anyone else in their friend group because she was afraid they would take Jennifer's side.

Sighing, she went into the kitchen to talk to her mom. She really hoped her mom would just listen this time. Sometimes she had a tendency to overreact.

"Mom, can we talk?" asked Erin.

Grace happily replied, "Sure sweetie, what do you want to talk about?"

Erin couldn't believe how nervous she was. She knew she could talk to her mom, but sometimes her mom could be hard to talk to. "Well, I really like this boy at school."

"You're too young to date," Grace replied with the same tired response Erin had heard over and over again. This was not going how she wanted.

"Moooom!"

"Sorry, go on," Grace waved her hand to have Erin continue.

"But I think he likes Jennifer, and she's been flirting with him—"

Interrupting Erin, Grace asked, "Does Jennifer know you like him?"

Erin didn't know what this had to do with anything and wanted to roll her eyes, but answered, "Yes, she's my best friend. I tell her everything."

"Why that little…"

With a huff Erin said, "Never mind," and walked away.

Grace said to her retreating back, "What did I do?"

What did this mother do? She didn't really listen or pay attention to her daughter's non-verbal cues. While her daughter started the conversation with "can we talk," in teen speak what she really wanted was her mom to listen.

OOOOOOOOOOOOOOOOOOOOOOOOOOO

Would you classify yourself as a good listener? Would your friends and family agree?

To truly be a good active listener you have to keep your mind clear, your ears open and your mouth shut, until it is your turn to speak.

The 1994 movie *Pulp Fiction* has a deleted scene in which Mia is filming Vincent. The dialogue is as follows.

Mia: "In conversation, do you listen or wait to talk?"

Vincent: "I have to admit that I wait to talk, but I'm trying harder to listen."

What about you? Do you feel like you listen or wait to talk?

I'll admit there are many times when I have caught myself or have been caught interrupting others because my brain is moving too fast. I don't usually do it intentionally, but the words are out of my mouth, and then I find myself apologizing for interrupting, or on some occasions, not realizing I have even done so. I've tried to get better about this and be more conscious of it.

Listening to a teenager is a little bit different than trying to listen to an adult because teenagers hear things differently than adults do. They need to feel that they're being heard in a different way. They'll often say, "you didn't hear me, you didn't hear what I said," or "you didn't listen to what I said to you." You may truly have been listening, but I have learned through my work with NLP (neuro-linguistic programming) that "my communication is the response I get." In this context, if your teen is responding with the responses above then there has been a breakdown in communication, and you need to come at it in a different way. Sometimes this can be as simple as repeating back what they said in your response. Sometimes it is not saying anything at all and just listening and nodding, sometimes it is saying something simple like, "I obviously misunderstood, could you please explain it to me again?" The idea is to validate, not argue.

OOOOOOOOOOOOOOOOOOOOOOOOOOO

When you signed up to be a parent did you know that you also signed up to be a reader of minds and body language and a foreign language translator?

Teenagers accuse parents of not listening to them. Sometimes they mean this literally, as adults are guilty of not paying attention just like the teens themselves are; however, the expectation is that you must also be able to read all the subtle distinctions of body language, know what is going on in their heads without them saying anything, and not only keep up with all the slang they might spew at you, but also know that they may have taken the words said to them differently than intended.

Tired yet?

Don't worry. It's not as complicated as that sounded, but that's how your teenager also sees life. Life is often overwhelming. It's often emotional. It's often frustrating. It is your job as a parent to try to help them feel less so by communicating with them in a way that makes them feel less overwhelmed, safe, and understood. These are words that repeatedly come up in responses from teenagers when asked what parents can do to help teenagers.

So, how do you do that? You must read your teenager. You must listen beyond the words they say and don't say. Many parents feel attacked if their teens hurl insults at them, and many parents feel attacked if their teens ignore them. More often than not, neither has anything to do with the parent. It's the age-old conundrum: you attack those that you know won't leave you. Now this isn't always the case. Some teens truly are angry at their parents, but most of the time it has more to do with what is going on internally than what is going on externally. If you feel like you are being beaten up emotionally as a parent, you may need to step away both physically and mentally and take this behavior with a grain of salt. Remember this treatment is about the teen, their world, and their issues. It usually has nothing to do with the parent. Except when it does.

Remember when we were discussing the teenage brain? Those emotional centers are rearing their ugly heads again.

I asked my students one day if they had a good relationship with their parents. Then I asked those that said no, what would make their relationship with their parents better? One of them said, "just listening and not like always having an opinion perhaps" and then I asked those that did why they thought they had a good relationship? One of them said, "We just don't argue much, they listen."

Listening often involves hearing from their perspective. What does this mean? Have you ever had one of those arguments with your child where you were saying the exact same thing they were saying but were still fighting? This may also involve letting them make their own mistakes regarding issues that don't matter much. The one's that aren't life and death. It may also involve not getting frustrated when someone else says the exact same thing in the exact same way you just did, and *your* child thinks the idea is brilliant.

In her book *One Trusted Adult*, Brooklyn Rainey tells a story of her son getting in trouble for having a vape pen at school. Her husband tells her son, "You are the company you keep. Is purchasing a vape pen a determining factor of the rest of your life? Not necessarily, but being a kid who vapes will determine the type of people you hang out with, and those people will determine how your network grows... the people you start spending time with now could have a huge impact on what direction your life goes." Her son didn't really have a reaction to this. However, his drum teacher offered to talk to him to see if he could have an impact. When asked about it, her son's response was, "it was awesome… He also told me that this choice doesn't define who I am, but it can determine the type of people I will end up surrounding myself with. So, I need to really think about who I want to be, and then I need to surround myself with people like that. Jared just really gets me."

Rainey thought her husband's head was going to explode because he thought he had just said the exact same thing, but her son didn't hear it that way because it came from a parent and not a trusted mentor.

The point: you need to find out what they heard you say and then don't argue about it. Validate what they heard you say, apologize for the misunderstanding, and try a different approach.

Listening also involves looking for external clues: body language. Have you ever agreed with someone but found yourself shaking your head no or clenching your fists or crossing your arms in a defensive posture because you didn't really agree? This can be either a conscious or unconscious act. Teenagers speak a lot with their body language. Take the dreaded eye roll as one example. The slouched posture can also be an indicator that something is wrong. You don't have to force them to sit up straight, although it is better for their mood and their posture to do so.

Sometimes, you will find your teen hanging around in the background. They may not initially feel comfortable engaging with the activity you are doing. But if you casually invite them to join you, they may actually do so. If you are cooking, "wanna help?" If you are watching TV, "wanna watch?" or "wanna pick something to watch together?" This way they feel like they can join or not, but they also feel wanted and not as uncomfortable. Teens often have trouble making eye contact with adults as well. If you want to engage them in conversations, take a car ride or go for a walk or a bike ride. Some activity where eye contact is not necessary for the conversation to occur.

Listening also involves making sure you understand what your teen is actually saying. This may be asking them to explain one of their slang words. For example, today I had to ask my teenagers to explain to me what a "bot" was. I asked them to explain it to me in adult speak. Basically, it is someone who does stupid "stuff."

The use of the words for what teenagers say when they are dating can cause misunderstandings as well. Back in the day they would say they were courting or going steady. I know when I used to talk to my mom about my friends that were dating, I would say they were going out, and she would ask me where they were going. I would roll my eyes at her like I couldn't believe she didn't understand.

The word dope used to mean cool; now it has a totally different meaning. The first time a student told me I was lit, I freaked out. I thought they were accusing me of being high. In fact, they were paying me a huge compliment. They were using it much the same way we used to use "dope." What is it with words that are associated with drugs through the years also being connected with being cool?

Tim McGraw has a song called "Back When." In the chorus to this song, he goes through an entire list of words like this. If you are familiar with this song, you know what I'm talking about. If not, look it up; you'll not only get a laugh, but you'll be reminded of why keeping up with the teenage lingo is so important.

Making sure you understand what your teenagers are talking about is only one part of this.

I watch for reactions in my classroom. I can often see when a student has shut down. I don't always know the reason, but I can see it. I am lucky that some of the students come to see me, and I get to learn more about them than just what I see in the classroom.

Throughout my experience with teenagers, it is the boys that I have had to watch the most carefully. Girls tend to emote more than boys, although there are some girls who will keep their emotions close to the vest as well.

I have always made my classroom a safe place where students can come and be themselves no matter what that entails.

One of the students I got to create this safe space for wrote this for me:

"High school was very long and complicated for me. I had half of my junior year over and graduated with the class below my original one. I spent a lot of my time either hiding in the counselor's office, the nurse's office or seeking oasis with Ms. Jass. I would eat lunch there and we would talk about my day and how I was emotionally and physically doing. She would always keep things straight for me. I was and still am a disabled young black queer adult and trying to be the true you in high school was very hard. We would talk about my fears and how it was so hard for me to make friends and fit in. She told me fitting in is overrated and being myself is what others wish they had the courage to do. Her classroom was a safe space where people could just be people as long as they weren't jerks."

For some students it was a place to vent with words, for others it was a place to come and just be able to yell and scream without being judged. For others they needed a physical outlet, and I let them bang on a wall. They just need a place to be themselves.

Often the trigger for the boys is a girl, just like for the girls it is a boy. Many boys are taught they can't get emotional. But they can't hold it all in either. Boys need to be taught it is okay to cry. It is okay to grieve. It is okay to let you know they might not be okay.

I have one student who shuts down completely when a relationship ends or there is something going on at home. He will not do work. He puts his head down in class. He acts like a jerk, but he will come in after school and talk about it. I can always tell when something is going on because of his body language in class. He feels he has a lot of weight on his shoulders at home, and you can practically see the weight on him. He doesn't know how to handle it. We are working on this together. I am teaching him some skills on how to cope both in school and at home. For this kid the name of the game is distraction and re-focus, but each teen is different. You have to know how they deal with anxiety and stress in order to know how to teach them to cope. This is why it is so important to "listen" to all aspects of your teen.

I had another student who tried to bottle up his emotions. He was on edge and would lash out at people. So much so that the nurse was worried for me when I took him into my classroom to talk. I let him vent. He talked, he punched the wall a few times, and then he broke down in tears, sliding down the wall. He felt like his world was ending. His pregnant girlfriend had broken up with him. That's a lot for a teenager to carry around, but people were more concerned about his behavior than his emotions. By letting him release some of those emotions, he was able to talk about the hurt beneath the anger. It released the steam from the pressure cooker.

So why do I tell you these stories? The idea is to pay attention. Paying attention to the words that your teenager is saying is not enough. What does your teen's body language tell you? How does your teen react when going through times of high emotion? If your teen is withdrawn, what other clues are there? What's underneath the surface emotion?

ᴑᴑᴑᴑᴑᴑᴑᴑᴑᴑᴑᴑᴑᴑᴑᴑᴑᴑᴑᴑᴑᴑᴑᴑᴑᴑᴑᴑᴑᴑ

Teens want more than anything to be seen. Many parents dread these teen years because of the emotional turmoil they know is coming. Dr. Kenneth Ginsburg was interviewed on the *Spawned Parenting* podcast answering the question "What if we lived in a society where the teen years weren't dreaded by the parents?" His answer was so enlightening. He says,

> "Right now if you Google "How do I talk to my kid?" the word that's most likely to come up is survival. This is poison. Poison because your child is about to enter this incredible moment where they're going to be changing, and where they're going to be figuring out who they are. Remember their fundamental question is "Who am I?" and what is going to get them through this period of time is having someone completely stable in their life who sees them the way they deserve to be seen and all of their goodness and all of their curiosity and celebrates that and if instead, they have

a sense when they're tweens that their mother and their father dread their development, and are going to react to their every mood in a way that's negative and undermining, we are actually shutting down the most protective force in young people's lives. The most protective force in their lives is parents who believe in them unconditionally, who see them as they deserve to be seen, and who always will stand by them, even if your teen walks out the room and slams the door."

Let's focus on Ginsburg's message for a minute. What they need from you is stability in a time in their life when they are not stable. They are growing, changing, figuring themselves out. They need you to believe in them unconditionally, to see them, and stand by them. Even when they are being real pains in the patooties. This is the time to listen with your heart, even when your heart may be taking a beating because your teen might have the emotional sensitivity of a gnat.

This does not mean you let them walk all over you. Boundaries are important.

What You Can Do as a Parent?

- Listen with your head, heart, eyes, and your ears.
- Validate your teen.
- Let them make mistakes that they can learn from.
- Keep up on the teen lingo.
- Set clear boundaries.

CHAPTER 5

WORKING ON BEING A GOOD COMMUNICATOR

———

It was my student teaching year. I had assigned lunch detention to one of my students in hopes of getting her to start turning in her work and inspiring her to turn her grade around. I have always been one to talk with my hands, to be expressive, to put a lot of emotion into my words. This day was no different. This student sat in the desk in front of me. I sat backwards on the desk facing her with my feet on the chair.

"What do you want to do with your life?"

"I want to be pregnant by the time I'm sixteen."

I tried not to react.

In my heart of hearts, I wanted so much more for her, not because I didn't see her being an amazing mother, not that being a mother couldn't be her goal, but I wanted so much for her to finish high school, for her to get her diploma, for her to have choices.

I pontificated, I waved my hands around, I explained to her all that she could have if she would just keep pushing forward, get her grades up. I told her how smart she was, how amazing a human being she was, and then, because as luck would have it there were no front legs on this desk that I had chosen to sit on, I proceeded to fall ass over tea kettle to the floor, the desk coming with me.

This lovely child laughed. She helped me up. We righted the desk.

Then she hugged me and said, "Ms. Jass, I love you. I want to introduce you to my brother when he gets out of jail."

The bell rang, and she left with a smile on her face.

I take two things from this embarrassing moment. The first is the fact that she thought enough of me to want to make me a part of her family even though I was lecturing her about her future. You can speculate about the second thing.

I realize looking back that my tactics were not the best. My heart was in the right place, my intentions were good, and I know she recognized how much I cared, but I don't think she heard a word I said. Even though she did end up doing better in school and graduating from high school without getting pregnant.

Celeste Hadlee would scold me for my pontificating and for not listening. Her TED talk, "10 Ways to Have a Better Conversation" would've helped me a lot back then. Number two of her ten ways is "Don't pontificate." Hadlee says, "You need to go into every conversation assuming that you have something to learn" and quotes famed therapist M. Scott Peck who said, "true listening requires a setting aside of oneself." Without the ability to set your own ego aside, true listening just cannot occur.

ᙁᙁᙁᙁᙁᙁᙁᙁᙁᙁᙁᙁᙁᙁᙁᙁᙁᙁᙁᙁ

Don't you just love those little moments that your teenager gives you where you feel like everything is going to be okay? Maybe they share with you what happened at school that day, or they had a bad day, and they need a hug, or they come to you while you are sitting on the couch and they sit next to you and put their head on your shoulder like they used to, or they ask for your advice about a problem they are having, or they want you to go somewhere with them. It could be any little scrap of attention or communication, but you take whatever you can get, and you cling to it because it feels like a lifeline in the sea of teenage emotional tug-of-war.

Some of you may be lucky enough to have your teens talk to you on a regular basis, but sometimes it is the attitude, tone of voice, or maybe you are just looking for further ways to strengthen your relationship. Whatever has brought you to this book, this chapter is one of the most important in terms of shifting the way you think about communicating with your teen. However, these strategies will also work with everyone in your life.

The old adage says, "communication is a two-way street." It is important to recognize that being present with your teens needs to be intentional.

One important thing to realize when dealing with your teens is you are also most likely activating things from your past that are driving your emotional grid. Sometimes this is done subconsciously. The way you were treated by your own parents, for example, influences the way you treat your children both positively and negatively. It can also manifest itself consciously as well. Think about times when you have said or have heard other parents say things like, "I remember what it was like to be a teenage boy, you are so not going to that party," or "I used to be a teenage boy, so I know what they were thinking."

Keith Hawkins, a motivational speaker for parents and teens, shared his experiences as a parent with me. He spoke of how both his wife and his upbringing influenced their own parenting. He grew up in a home where "children were to be seen and not heard" while his wife grew up in a home where they listened to her, her opinion mattered, and they validated her. He finds himself drifting towards the way he was brought up and tries to be conscious of that, so he can change it. Once you become mindful of these things you can make a conscious effort to make your child raising better than your own. Hawkins says "that's what I'm doing right now. My wife and I have paid attention to that and I've gotten much better because I've identified it. I've owned it, and I've set goals to be responsible and make it better not just knowing it, but taking actions." For him some of these actions were to listen, to give them space, to give them a voice.

Learning how to recognize that you are doing this and actively separate yourself from putting these past emotions on your child is important in creating positive communication channels with your teen.

〇〇〇〇〇〇〇〇〇〇〇〇〇〇〇〇〇〇〇〇〇〇〇〇〇〇〇〇〇〇〇〇

Celeste Hadlee's TED talk "10 Ways to Have a Better Conversation," identifies some other important things to pay attention to when having a conversation with anyone, let alone your teenager. Number one is "Don't multitask." She is not just talking about putting away your cell phone. The idea is to be in the moment, to truly be present. This is so important with your teens. They will feel it with their spidey senses if you are distracted. Number four ties directly to this one: "go with the flow." As ideas come into your mind, let them go. Don't get distracted from what your teen is saying. Stay in the moment.

With number five, Hadlee reminds us adults of something very important when dealing with teens, even though she wasn't talking directly about teens, "it's okay to say I don't know." If you don't know the answer, just say so, or say you'll find out, or even search for the answer with your teen, depending on the topic. They will respect your honesty more than you making something up.

Again, Hadlee makes a truly valid point with number six, "don't equate your experience with theirs." To a teenager this is the equivalent of "when I was your age," but as human beings our experiences are our own. Unless your teen asks, let them tell you about their experience. It is not about you, or how you handled a similar experience, or even that you know what they are going through.

No matter who you are trying to communicate with it is important to build rapport. Rapport is that close connection with another person, the feeling that you are in harmony with one another. You know, that feeling that you just click. You understand each other's feelings and ideas and communicate easily.

But how do you build rapport?

Some rapport with your teen will be natural because you are the parent and there is an inherent sense of trust and safety. However, if you have broken your child's trust in any perceived way, your rapport may be out of harmony.

One way to get into rapport with your teen (or anyone else for that matter) is what neurolinguistic programming

(NLP) calls mirroring and matching. Observe your teen's breathing, the subtle movements they are making, their mannerisms, then subtly mirror and match these in pace, tone and rhythm (it should not be distinct enough that they feel you are mimicking them). By doing this, your teen will begin to feel a strong closeness to you even if they are not aware you are mirroring and matching. This technique allows you to enter your teen's map of the world.

Entering your teen's map of the world is essential for building rapport. What is this map that I speak of? This is our perception of the world. Reality has very little to do with the way we perceive the world because our memories are faulty at best. If I asked you and your teen to describe an experience that you both went through in the past, both of you would have similar details, but your memories would be shaped by your own experiences. Your teenager is experiencing life very differently than you are. It is important to take the time to view life through their map as it exists now if you want to be able to have open dialogue.

This can be done from a distance, but try this activity, if your teen is open to it. It will allow both you and your teen to experience each other's map of the world in a unique way.

Go somewhere where you can walk around and interact with the environment and people: a park, the mall, the zoo, an amusement park, the beach, a hiking trail, your neighborhood, etc.

Pick who goes first. Then follow the other person and mirror and match what the other person does. If your teen texts on her phone, you mirror texting on your phone. If they are swinging their arms, you swing your arms. Mirror posture, walking stride, whether looking down, up, side to side, talking to people (although you can mime this if you want to keep the embarrassment to a minimum).

Do this for ten minutes and switch. Then talk to each other about how it felt and what you learned about both yourself and your teen. You can do this with other members of your family as well. I know every time I do this activity, I learn a lot about not only the partner I worked with, but I also learn new things about myself as well. I love hearing stories about what other people learn from this activity. It's one of my favorites.

The first time I did this activity was at my transformational leader Niurka's course, Supreme Influence in Action (SIIA). We were at a hotel in Palm Springs, CA. My partner stopped briefly to look at an herb garden. I found myself wanting to interact more with the herb garden, but my partner smelled one of the plants and moved on. The herb garden had captured my partner's attention enough to make her stop, but it didn't hold her interest for long. When it was my turn, I went back to the herb garden, which I would never even have known about had it not been for my partner's exploration and spent more time there. I wanted to know which herbs were in the garden, I wanted to see if we were allowed to pick them (the answer was "no" and even though I was tempted to pick them anyway, I didn't.) In our conversation that followed, the herb garden hadn't even registered on my partner's radar other than she thought it was cool that a hotel had an herb garden. But she was fascinated by my spending so much time there and she found herself being more curious about the herbs afterwards. I was also surprised by my fascination with the herb garden as I am not a gardener. My mom is the gardener in our family. It would have made her happy to know that I was drawn to green things.

The point of the above story is to show you the types of things you can learn about people when you take the time to immerse yourself in their view of the world. My partner went from the herb garden to the pool. She was from a place where it is cold most of the year and wanted to bask in the California sunshine in February. Putting her feet in the pool knowing it was snowing at home made her very happy. Contentment oozed from her as I mirrored and matched her, and while I often take the California sunshine for granted, I really enjoyed it that day.

The more you know about your teen, the more help you can give them. Using what you already know about them is vital as well.

OOOOOOOOOOOOOOOOOOOOOOOOOOOOOO

You know your teen better than anyone else. They ask you a question. You say, "No." They come back with, "But why can't I..." It doesn't matter what they have asked, or what you have said no to. They always want to know why you have said no. I bet your instinct is usually to say, "Because I said so." This is absolutely true, and you could say this. I know my parents said this at least a time or two or ten during my childhood, but I would say that a true explanation of why you are saying no would go a lot further in keeping the lines of communication open between you and your teen, even if they still don't like the response.

Mayim Bialik who many of you may know as the actress from *Big Bang Theory* is also a neuroscientist. She wrote two books called *Boying Up* and *Girling Up*. In these books, she talks directly to the boys and girls she writes the books for. In each book, she addresses the issue of why parents don't allow their children to watch certain movies or television shows. Her explanations are something I think parents could benefit from in addressing questions of why you are saying no. When addressing the girls in *Girling Up*, Bialik tells them, "It is the job of parents to protect children from things that might upset them or hurt them or introduce them to concepts that they are just not ready for. This might be why your parents don't let you watch a certain kind of movie or TV show. They may have knowledge of ways you have reacted to similar things in the past, and they may not feel that you're ready to handle something until you have a bit more knowledge and maturity." She adds in *Boying Up* that she often tells her own sons, "there are certain things that exist in the world that are really intense and that, once you see them, you can't unsee them." She uses example questions such as "have you ever watched a movie or a TV show that makes you feel sad and emotional, but you watched it with a friend who had absolutely no reaction to it? Have you ever seen something in a movie or on TV that was really upsetting and made your stomach hurt, but other people who saw it didn't find it upsetting at all? How about this: have you ever seen something on the news that made a friend of yours feel yucky and grossed out, but you felt totally fine about it?" She explains the reasons for this as "everyone has different levels of sensitivity to different things" because of genetics. It isn't right or wrong. People are just different.

I always think about horror movies when I read this. Maybe your child had nightmares when they watched something scary, or they reacted badly in real life to scary things. You are protecting them by not allowing them to watch a scary movie until you feel they are ready.

Bialik says a couple of other things that are both important and helpful:

1. In *Boying Up,* she says, "What many parents know, and what we often don't get when we are not yet parents, is that all of the movies and TV shows we watch add to our learning because the things we see and experience when we watch movies and TV become a part of our brains and, in some way, make up who we are for the rest of our lives."

2. In *Girling Up,* Bialik focuses on how parents might want to keep their young girls away from things that promote negative body image. In *Boying Up,* she focuses on the fact that movies, TV, and the media give boys the idea what is the norm in terms of things like women, sex, and drugs. She says, "Parents often want to wait until your brain has developed a bit more before letting you see all of that, since early exposure to this kind of stuff can make your brain have expectations about what's normal, even if it's not normal or healthy."

All of these issues are useful ways to address with your teens the reasons why you won't allow them to watch certain movies or TV shows or go to a concert or even allow them on social media. Rather than just saying "no" or "because I said so." When you put it in these contexts, it allows your teen a way to understand where you are coming from even if they still don't like it. They may still pout, roll their eyes, give you the silent treatment, or any number of those wonderful teenage attitudes, but they will (maybe deep down) respect you more for the explanation.

Not only is what teens see and do important, the words we speak also have a power of their own.

OOOOOOOOOOOOOOOOOOOOOOOOOOOOOO

"Sticks and stones may break my bones, but words will never hurt me." The greatest lie ever told to and by children everywhere. While true in that words cannot cause physical harm, the psychological damage that words can do is life altering.

The power of words is undeniable. As an English teacher, this has been a theme throughout my units for many years. Words have the power to lift us up and they have the power to cut us down.

When we talk about the power of words in my classroom, I ask my students:

"How many words does it takes to ruin your day?"

A chorus of, "one."

Then I ask them, "How many does it take to fix it?"

A chorus of, "a lot."

Once ruined, it takes a lot to fix the damage.

Sometimes a simple "I love you" repairs damage, but even those words can become meaningless if abused.

Your teenagers are listening to every word you say even if they pretend they are not. They need your praise more than your criticism, although this does not mean they do not need guidance and discipline.

What Can You Do as a Parent?

- Be Present.
- Build Rapport.
- Share your experiences but don't equate your experiences with theirs.
- Give more praise than criticism.

CHAPTER 6

QUESTIONS ARE THE ANSWERS

———

Monica enters the school pickup line. Her son Andrew is exiting the school building with his friends. Her heart soars. He is laughing and joking with his friends. She is hopeful that this means the conversation in the car will go better today than it has in the past.

Andrew climbs in the car, takes his phone out of his pocket and puts his ear buds in. He slouches down in his seat. Monica deflates. She wonders what happened to the boy who was just laughing and joking with his friends.

She tries to keep her voice upbeat as she taps him on the shoulder and motions for him to remove his earbuds. He takes one out.

Monica: How was your day?

Andrew: Fine.

Monica: Just fine.

Andrew nods

Monica: What did you do?

Andrew: Went to class.

Monica: Did anything exciting happen?

Andrew: Not really.

Monica sighs and starts the car. Andrew puts his earbud back in and turns back to his phone. He shoots a text to whoever is on the other end of the device and chuckles slightly at the response he gets. He doesn't look at her the entire ride home. The only sound in the car is the beat Monica can hear from Andrew's earbuds. She could turn the radio on, but Andrew would just ask her to turn it off. Been there done that. Rinse. Repeat.

Monica was not wrong to ask Andrew questions. However, these questions did not interest Andrew, so he did not engage. No matter what the age, questions need to provoke.

Young children are curious. They ask lots of questions. Do you remember when your child went through the "why" phase? It's about that time when most parents start thinking "we spent all that time waiting for them to talk and now we wish they had an off button." There's a documentary on Apple+ called *Becoming You* that traces the development of children from birth to the age of five. It discusses children all around the world. It shows that there are certain stages that all children go through no matter how they are raised or where they are from. This stage of curiosity is one of them. In the last episode of the series, twin three-year-old boys incessantly ask their mother "why" as they walk to the butterfly garden. The mother takes the time to patiently answer all of their questions. Did you know that children this age can ask up to seventy-five questions an hour and that between the ages of two and five they will ask approximately 40,000 questions? Most of the time these children really do want to know the answers to the questions they ask and if you as the parent do not take the time to satisfy their curiosity, they will keep asking. There are two powerful drives behind these questions: it boosts knowledge and the thought of finding out something new actually makes them feel good.

I was one of these very curious children. I always asked a lot of questions, and some of these questions seemed to be mature questions for my age. My mom had a saying, "if she's old enough to ask the question, she's old enough to know the answer… but only to the question she's asking." Meaning that she didn't elaborate unless I asked further questions. She also made sure I really did want to know the answers to the questions I was asking. Sometimes, the answer was no, I did not.

Children tend to be happy with the simple answers. They may ask for more information or they may move on, but it isn't always necessary to give all the details. For example, if a young child asks, "where do babies come from?" It isn't necessary to give them an entire sex education lesson. You may be able to simply say, "from mommy's tummy."

The same can be true for teenagers. They actually ask less questions because they think they know everything, but in reality, they only know what they know. They apply their limited life experiences and what is in their world, namely what they have learned so far from school, family, friends, and social media to everything that happens to them. Teenagers seem to know everything and that their parents are wrong most of the time, until something directly impacts them to show them they may not know as much as they think they do.

One of the best ways to approach teenagers is to ask them questions. Questions really do become the answer. However, the intent behind the question matters.

Teenagers can sniff out what Holden Caulfield called "phoniness" in *The Catcher in the Rye* and will resent you for your lack of honesty. They want you to show that you are invested in them and what they care about.

This applies to the type of questions you ask them as well.

As I am writing this book, my students have just finished a year full of hybrid and distance learning due to the COVID-19 pandemic. Many of them struggled with school; however, they have had a big part in the creation of this book, and I gave them questionnaires to fill out that also connected to units we discussed in class. Even students who did no other work for me completed these questionnaires. Why? Because it mattered to them. They want someone to listen to them about issues that relate to and impact their lives directly.

It's the same if you want to get answers from your teens. These teens have decided that adults no longer have the right to ask questions or if we do, we are being annoying.

Dr. Lisa Damour discusses this issue of questions in her book *Untangled*. She also went to the source and asked the teenage girls she works with how parents, and adults in general, can ask non-annoying questions. What she found beyond this idea of honesty was this: "A girl will reject a question if she suspects the parent doesn't really care about the answer and has asked just to try to connect. And girls don't like questions designed to pry." So, what do girls want? According to Damour, "Girls want questions driven by genuine interest." Don't ask "how was your day?" Instead "ask about something specific that you really want to know." And if she changes the direction of the conversation, let her. If you remember she mentioned something last week, ask about it with the same language she used, so she knows you don't have an angle. Damour says, "Girls tell me that they want their parents to pick up the conversational topics they put on the table... Should she volunteer that her band teacher seems to have gotten crankier try, "Really? What kind of cranky?" or "Huh, any idea what's going on?"

So, what about boys? Damour's book specifically deals with girls because her audience is girls, but I've seen the same thing in the boys I've spoken with too. Most of the strategies above will work with boys as well. In fact, honesty might be more important to them. If a boy is willing to talk, let him talk and definitely make sure to ask questions about what he has brought up.

Dr. Kenneth Ginsburg offered this advice on the *Spawned Parenting* podcast, "if you ask grilling questions that are about personal subjects, then you're actually entering territory that teenagers don't think parents have a right to be in." He doesn't recommend starting with questions or comments like "tell me about your friends" or "tell me about why you're wearing this." Not if you want an answer. But if you start with questions that stretch their mind, things that will provoke their opinion, offer to have them teach you something. What do you think about this? What's your opinion? Teach me about this. What is it like out there right now for young people? Then they are the ones driving the conversation instead of feeling like they are being grilled, and you avoid the one word or short responses like in the example at the beginning of the chapter. Ginsburg also suggests, "go drive, walk down the street and notice things around you and talk about that, because when your sentences don't begin with, what are you doing, but they begin with, what do you think's happening over there, you learn your child's opinions, you gain their wisdom, and you learn all about them without being direct."

One of my students offered her own advice on questions to ask. "Often asking questions such as 'Are you okay?' and 'What can I do to help you?' go a long way. Sometimes teenagers merely want their parents' presence, which in my experience helps a lot. Just knowing they're there if I need them is more than enough."

Be careful of where you are asking questions as well as how often you are asking them. If you ask questions in front of others, you risk embarrassment. Sometimes the number of questions can be overwhelming and intrusive too. In a conversation, one parent told me this story, "I have a relative that fires questions so fast you think you're being interrogated by the police. He has a teen and his daughter answered him one day by saying she feels she is being judged by him when all these questions get fired at her in the kitchen surrounded by her huge extended family. She let him know how she felt right in front of everyone, then glanced over at me with a face as if pleading for help. I spoke with the father in private and suggested he apologize and they discuss this further in private. It helped, but this guy still needs to watch his style of questioning as I have had to tell him the same thing about how he even treats me—an adult—like this and it is super intrusive to the point of being annoying. So bottom line, these questions must be asked with respect and gentleness and not from the standpoint of 'I'm your father, I'm the boss, I'm over you in the pecking order.'" Throwing your weight around as a parent to get answers will further isolate you from your teen. This will keep them from coming to you rather than what you really want, which is for them to want to share with you of their own free will.

Some parents use questions to probe for information in an attempt to protect their children, but it can become like an interrogation and cause your teen to shut down rather than open up. Kenneth, Ilana, and Talia Ginsburg in their book *Raising Kids to Thrive* remind us, "it's not what we *ask;* it is what we *know.* When we ask a lot of questions, the answers are not always truthful. To effectively monitor our children, we want to be the kinds of parents to whom kids choose to disclose what is going on in their lives."

What happens when you don't get a response? Have you taught your child the saying, "if you don't have anything nice to say, don't say anything at all"? Their silence might be them trying to maintain some type of respect because they know what will come out of their mouth is not what should.

There is no reason for you to be treated with disrespect; however, the word respect holds a lot of weight with teenagers. Adults keep telling them that adults deserve respect. Respect your elders and all that, but teenagers feel like they should be shown respect as well, and they aren't always necessarily wrong. It is how they define respect that sometimes muddies the waters with adults.

Lisa Damour said something in *Untangled* that I really support. She said that, at a minimum, you should expect your [child] to be polite. She also says, "I can be polite to people who don't earn my respect" and I agree that "this is as much as we should expect our [children] to do." If you can't respect your elders, can you at least be polite to them? You might even actually pose this question to your teen. The word choice is important. Focusing on politeness might just be enough to trigger a change, at least until they truly feel that you have earned their respect.

None of my advice is about letting your teens walk all over you. They don't want to. They will respect you more when there is some form of discipline when they have done something wrong. Even if it is just being called out for their rudeness. Remember, calling someone out does not have anything to do with yelling or a raised voice or a stern tone or even a glare. Truth can still be told with a gentle and quiet tone of voice.

What Can You Do As a Parent?

- Ask questions that matter to your teen.
- Ask questions that require your teen's opinion.
- Be conscious of where you are when you ask questions.
- Don't grill your teen. Gentle probing questions will get better results.

CHAPTER 7

IT ALL DEPENDS ON YOUR PERSPECTIVE

———

I was on Facebook and saw this conversation posted by a mother that had occurred between her and her teenage daughter.

Mother: "I like your new shirt."

Daughter: "You can't wear it."

Mother: "I don't want to wear it."

Daughter: "Then why did you say you like it?!"

Mother: "Because it looks lovely on you."

Daughter: "Then you do like it… but you still can't wear it."

Mother: "I don't want to wear it."

Daughter: "It won't look as good on you and you're too old for a shirt like this…"

Mother: "*I don't want to wear it!!!!!*"

Daughter: "Yes you do… you said you like it."

skips away

Mother: "Aaaaarrrrrgggghhh!!!"

If you are a mother of a teenage daughter reading this, you most likely had some reaction to reading this. Your reaction will likely depend on the actual familiarity you have with this type of conversation with your own daughter. If you had a visceral reaction to this, I feel for you. If you laughed out loud, believe me you will have some type of conversation akin to this with your teen at some point before they leave adolescence.

Why do conversations like this occur? Are teenagers just trying to be difficult? Some may be, but for the most part, conversations with your teens that end with you shaking your head and wondering where the miscommunication occurred are the product of communication occurring on different wavelengths.

The adult in you read the totally innocent first line where the mother stated, "I like your new shirt" and probably thought the mother was innocently complimenting the daughter, unless you had a mother or sibling who constantly borrowed your clothes, in which case you may have been in the small minority who thought the same thing the daughter did.

I think my favorite part of this whole exchange is that the daughter doesn't seem to get angry with the mother at all. She even "skips away." It is the mother who gets frustrated; that's why she is sharing the story on social media.

You may be wondering what to do in this situation. How do you avoid an innocent compliment from becoming something else? Because your child may not be as calm as this child seems to be.

The first step is acknowledging that this child is not wrong just because what she heard is not what the mother intended to say. This is all about perception. In her map of the world, this child heard her mother's "I like your shirt" as "I want to borrow your shirt."

The best way to find out how not to repeat this event again would be to go back to the idea of asking questions. Remember, questions are the answers, but it might take some time to get to that point. This doesn't mean you should not try.

Try something like this.

Mother: I would like to give you a compliment about your shirt without you thinking I want to wear your shirt. How would I go about doing that?

Whatever you do, don't engage in the old argument.

Your child may roll her eyes at you, or she may simply answer the question. Keep at it. The fact that you care to get clarification will register on some level.

ꝏꝏꝏꝏꝏꝏꝏꝏꝏꝏꝏꝏꝏꝏꝏꝏꝏ

Do you remember playing the telephone game as a kid? We'd all sit in a line, and someone would start by whispering something into the first person's ear and that person would whisper what they heard into the next person's ear and so on down the line until it got to the last person. Then the last person would say what they heard, and the first person would say what they'd actually said, and everyone would laugh because it was almost never the same, and the more people that were in the line, the farther from the original it would be.

Memory and perspective are a lot like this. Especially for teenagers. What you as the parent/adult see or hear is not always the same as what your teen does.

Recently, I attended an online conference for teachers, and Gerry Brooks, a principal from Lexington, KY, was giving the keynote speech. He said something very profound about perspective, "when you look through the lens of another person, you gain sympathy, empathy, and understanding." I want you to really think about this when dealing with your teen. Here's a personal example that I use with my senior students when trying to put them in your shoes. This is the how the story I share with them usually goes.

Me: Who do you think graduation is really for?

Student 1: Me.

Student 2: My parents.

Me: You're both right. Completing the course work to graduate is for you. Some of you need your diploma to get into college, some of you need it for your jobs, but all you need is your transcript or that piece of paper for that to happen. Most of you really just want to see your friends in your cap and gown, the pictures and the graduation parties, gifts, and money that come along with graduation. We call this the pomp and circumstance of it all.

(At this point, most of the students are agreeing with me.)

Me: Graduation is really for your parents. This is their accomplishment as much as yours. This is the point that they know they have raised you right and that you have done them proud. It doesn't really matter what your GPA is, although they do puff up more if you have asterisks by your name or you are wearing cords and such. But for the most part, they are just so proud that you are walking across that stage.

Some of the students nod in understanding. For some a light bulb goes on. For others, it still takes more work.

Then I tell them this story.

One year I got a phone call from a parent. She was concerned about whether or not her son was going to graduate. She said, "I have all of his graduation announcements addressed and in the envelopes, but I don't know if I can mail them."

I told her that her son knew exactly what he needed to do to pass my class. He didn't have a lot to do, he just needed to complete it and turn it in to me.

She thanked me and hung up.

I started thinking about this situation from her perspective. Imagine, if this was your mom, and she was out at the supermarket and she encountered another mom. This mom knows that her son is graduating from high school. She asks, "are you excited about your son's graduation?" She doesn't know if he is graduating. This puts this mother in an awkward position of either having to lie and say, "yes, I am so excited," or saying the truth, "I'm anxious as I don't know if he's going to graduate yet." Or even worse, if this happens after the graduation, and he didn't do the work, "my son didn't graduate" would be her response to anyone asking how the graduation was.

How would the mother feel?

Student 1: Embarrassed.

Me: Exactly.

Some of the students who are failing the class still wouldn't care, and then I try to put myself in their perspective and figure out why they don't care. For others, seeing this from the perspective of their parents is enough to get them motivated.

As a parent, ask yourself what is causing your teen to fail in the first place? Put yourself in their shoes. Not as a disciplinarian but as the teen themselves. Maybe they don't understand the work and are afraid to ask the teacher for help. Maybe they are so far behind they feel overwhelmed. In this case, don't blame them for getting to this point; find a strategy to help them out of it. See it from their point of view and come at it from a positive place rather than a negative one.

One of the presuppositions of NLP (neuro-linguistic programming) says there is no such thing as failure, only feedback. I have this quote hanging in my classroom. I think this is really important for teenagers. When something doesn't work, use the experience to figure out how to do it differently.

OOOOOOOOOOOOOOOOOOOOOOOOOOOOOOOO

In her book *Supreme Influence*, one of my mentors Niurka reminds us, "One of the greatest barriers to communication is assuming that it has happened!" If there is a misunderstanding in communication, own it. You are the adult. You have the experience. If a misunderstanding has occurred, regroup and try again... in a new way.

I attended a professional development workshop with Brian Mendler on engaging hard-to-reach students. He said something so profound, and it changed my perspective on engaging in arguments with my students. Basically, he told a group of educators we did not need to have the last word. As a parent, this is true for you as well.

The second to last word is best.

We are the adults.

We can walk away.

It is actually more powerful to do so because the children lose their ability to engage.

Mind blown.

This isn't really a huge deal, is it? But how many times do we continue to engage? Knowing when not to communicate is just as important as knowing when to communicate.

For some of you this will be the most difficult part to implement. I know there are times when I still have to remind myself to walk away. Sometimes you find yourself so deep in the argument you want to come out the victor. Sometimes you find yourself wondering in the middle of the argument how it even got started, but the point is not to win. The point is not to damage the relationship with the teen in your life. The point is to disengage from the argument and your teen with boundaries put in place, with an acceptable outcome, with results when necessary. This never ends well when two people are screaming at each other.

Brooklyn Raney, author of *One Trusted Adult* gives a great example of the difference between the adult and the teen perspective with a story about the word unpredictable. Her son told his nurse that his mother was unpredictable, leading the nurse to think she might be "neglectful and abusive." When Raney questions her son, he responds by saying "'If I break the rules, I have no idea if you aren't going to let me play video games, or if you are going to take my iPod away, or if I'm not going to get to go to a friend's house his weekend. Wouldn't you call that *unpredictable?*'" From his perspective, Raney's behavior *was* unpredictable. The unintended consequences of this misunderstanding could have been disastrous, but he wasn't necessarily wrong. In his definition, what happened was a misunderstanding; a breakdown in communication due to the way in which this teenager used the word unpredictable and the way the nurse perceived the meaning of his communication.

When I was young, we had a light hologram in our living room. It sat on a wooden pedestal and was taller than I was. I remember one day standing with my dad looking at the hologram with my dad. He pointed out a shape in it, but I told him I couldn't see it. He said, "What do you mean, it's right there?" He kept trying to explain to me where it was in the hologram, and I kept saying, "I don't see it." He was getting more and more frustrated thinking I was lying or messing with him. Then he finally got on his knees so that he was at my level and realized that the hologram had a totally different image at my level. His perspective was literally different than mine, and he was getting mad because we were truly not seeing eye to eye.

One of my twelfth-grade students had some advice to give on this subject of perspective. She said, "Just listen. Don't interrupt, don't try to make them see things through an 'adult' perspective. Just listen and try to see things through the perspective of the teenager, trusting you enough to vent, ask for help, from you. Just a teenager trusting you enough to ask for help is a big deal to them."

What Can You Do as a Parent?

- Take the time to look through your teen's perspective (sometimes both figuratively and literally).
- Don't engage in the old argument.
- Second to last word is best.

CHAPTER 8

ANXIETY AND MOTIVATION

It was two a.m., my dad was fuming as he stormed into his and my mother's room. "I'm going to kill her!" My dad growled.

When I was a teenager, like all other teens, I had a curfew. If I was going to be late, I had to call. One night, my parents came home and checked my room. They didn't see me. My dad sat on the couch waiting for me to come home. My curfew came and went and still he didn't see me come through the door. He waited… and waited, getting angrier by the minute.

My mom finally said to him, "Are you sure she isn't in her room?"

He gave her an incredulous look and said, "I already checked."

She went into my room and there I was asleep… under my comforter. I had been there the whole time. I had come home before they did, but my dad didn't come into my room; he just looked and couldn't see me under the comforter.

He assumed the worst.

The next morning, he told me the story. About how he was so angry he was ready to kill me. We laughed about it. We still laugh about it to this day.

But what was really driving his anger was his fear that something had happened to me. His anxiety about where I was, what was going on, and if I would come home safely.

I had never broken curfew, I had never not called, but a parent's anxiety and fear are not rational, and I understand this as an adult. Your teens will not necessarily understand this.

When your child was first born, you would do anything to protect them, right? They were so fragile. They relied on you for everything. Their first needs were simple, but also anything but. They needed clothing, feeding, changing and sleeping, but they also couldn't tell you if anything was wrong or exactly what they needed. New parents feel a range of emotions, but anxiety is often at the top of the list. Especially if it is your first child.

As your child continued to grow, you might have marveled at all that was learned, but the anxiety never really went away. They would get hurt and there was nothing you could do to stop it. They were little explorers figuring out the world. They would challenge you, surprise you, make you proud, make you laugh, a full range of emotions, but protection and keeping your child safe is always in the back of your mind, no matter how old they are.

The older your child gets, the more independent they become. The more autonomy they want. The more they say, "I can do it." You want to allow them to do more on their own, but they are still your baby, and you worry.

Then they become a teenager and this anxiety is ramped up. The world is a scary place. You put more rules into place. You warn them of all the dangers, but you worry it isn't enough.

Your teen gets into trouble.

You blame yourself.

But this anxiety does not have to be all-consuming.

Your teens are feeling anxiety at much the same level you are, if not more. They want to understand the world they are living in as much as you do. Together you can navigate some of the areas that may be causing undue anxiety for both of you.

If you are the father of a teenage daughter, you may remember what you were like as a teenager and use that to gauge the way you choose to allow your daughter to date. It may be conscious or unconscious. It may be valid, or it might not be, but understand that projecting your anxieties onto your daughter can do harm to her self-esteem. You don't have to allow her to date, but you should not say "I remember what boys were like at my age, and I am not letting them anywhere near you."

As the mother of a teenage son, you may want him to stay your baby boy forever, but he will want to become his own man, sometimes before you are ready, and you need to support him and encourage him to do just that.

Often as the mother of a daughter, your own insecurities may be projected onto your daughter. Fight this urge with all your might. You may not even be conscious of doing it, but if there is friction, this may be the cause.

The father of a son can raise a strong man and still show him how to have emotions beyond anger and a stiff upper lip.

I've told my own parents one of the things I think they did right was not fighting in front of us. I think throughout my whole childhood I remember hearing one fight between my mom and dad, and it was my mom fighting with my dad for something that mattered to me. As discussed in chapter two, the anxiety levels of teens are at an all-time high. Both children and adolescents are very in-tune to their surroundings, and they pick up on what is going on at home. You might not be able to hide the way that you feel, but you should try to keep the fighting behind closed doors.

Many of my students have expressed the desire to help their parents as much as their parents help them. They know when you are struggling. They want to lessen your burdens even if they don't show it. Whether you are in a healthy marriage and just have arguments or an unhealthy one that is leading to an eventual end, your children should not be the ones to suffer for it. It has a ripple effect.

Several of my students shared that they would rather keep their problems to themselves than share their burdens with their parents because their parents have enough on their plate. They don't want to add to their parents' anxiety. While they are listening to everything you say, they are also paying attention to all the other cues I have asked you to pay attention in them, like your body language and your actions.

In his interview on the *Spawned Parenting* podcast, Dr. Kenneth Ginsburg talks about two steps that parents need to really understand about why teens push parents away. This can really be anxiety-inducing for the parents.

"The first thing is understanding they're pushing you away because they love you. Why do you have to start there? Because you have to calm yourself... What you have to remember about adolescents is that they're deeply emotional... They're exuberant, they're social, they feel things fully... When a parent gets super emotional, when a parent gets super reactive, then the volume and the escalation just goes up. So, the first thing is to know where it comes from. The second is, give yourself some space, if you're feeling angry or you're feeling frustrated... give yourself space, and it's really okay to talk about it. So, if your kid's name is Susie, it's okay to go, Susie right now I'm feeling really angry, and I'm not in my best place to talk, and you wouldn't want to hear what I have to say, I'm going to go take a break. I'm going to go for a run, then we're going to talk afterwards. When you do that, you set yourself up for better communication later on, and you're teaching them how to self-regulate. You're modeling being human. And that's a great thing."

We are human. We have flaws. It is okay to both have them and show them. It does not make you weak in the eyes of your teen. It actually will make them relate to you more. The more candid you can be with your teen, the more honest and open they will be with you.

ꙨꙨꙨꙨꙨꙨꙨꙨꙨꙨꙨꙨꙨꙨꙨꙨꙨꙨꙨꙨꙨꙨ

In Dr. Lisa Damour's book *Under Pressure*, she tells the story of the glitter jar.

She also tells the story of her loathing of glitter, and I have to tell you that I share that loathing. Let me tell you the story first. When I moved into one of my new classrooms, I inherited a desk. This desk had previously belonged to a teacher who taught English and journalism. I repeat: English and journalism. As I was putting my stuff into the desk, I opened the bottom left-hand drawer and encountered something I would never have thought to find... almost an entire layer of loose *glitter* covering the bottom of the drawer. Those of you familiar with glitter know that no matter how much of the glitter I tried to dump or wipe out of this drawer, I found glitter on me until I got rid of that bloody desk. I still have no idea why the desk of a former English and journalism teacher had that much glitter in it, but it has left me with a loathing for the shiny, sticks-to-everything, stuff. My cousin and her daughter think it's quite amusing to buy me stuff with glitter on, in, and around it. Going so far as to buy me an entire jar of purple glitter!

So back to the glitter jar and why no matter that I have this loathing of glitter, I made my own glitter jar to take with me to my classroom. A glitter jar is a clear jar about four inches tall, filled with water, glitter glue, and a thick layer of glitter that sits on the bottom. The lid is secured with glue (Just know mine is uber secure. That lid will never come off.) There are many different recipes to be found online.

Damour got the idea from some of her colleagues at a girls' school in Dallas when they started talking about the turbulent emotions of teenage girls. The colleague told her that when a girl comes into her office in a panic, she will take out the glitter jar and shake it like a snow globe. Then she says to the girl, "'Right now, this is what it's like in your brain. So first, let's settle your glitter.'" Then she sets the jar down between them and they watch it until the glitter settles, giving the girl a chance to settle too.

This is not just good for the kids. It is good for you parents as well. One idea is to use it to take a moment when your conversation with your teen is going a little off the rails. Grab the glitter jar. Shake it up. Then wait for the glitter to settle before you continue your conversation. You could even each have your own jar. The shaking of the jar itself has a calming effect.

OOOOOOOOOOOOOOOOOOOOOOOOOOOOOOO

As a parent, your motivation is most often the safety of your child; secondly, the success of your child. Your teen may be intrinsically motivated, or it may be that trying to motivate your teen makes you feel a little like a Sisyphean task. For those of you not familiar with poor Sisyphus, he was one of those ancient Greeks who was punished and had to push a boulder up a hill only to have it keep rolling back down just when he felt like he was getting somewhere.

As a high school English teacher, I am constantly trying to find ways to motivate students. English and math are generally students' least favorite subjects. By the time they get to high school, most students hate both reading and writing. When I finally get a student who says that English is their favorite subject, I get a little giddy. It is usually because they love to read or write.

Motivating teens is something that I have been looking into for many years. I have gone to several professional development workshops and have read many books on the subject trying to figure out why many teens are so unmotivated.

I taught one year of seventh and eighth grade English. It was a very enlightening experience for me as I had only taught high school up to that point, and I had been teaching for seventeen years at the time. I had to dig deep and remember how I felt about my own middle school years in order to really appreciate the difference between the high school aged students and the middle school students. In reality, those years were for me a holding pattern, a time to wait for high school, but I was also intrinsically motivated. Even though I did not enjoy those years of school, I wouldn't settle for poor grades.

Middle schoolers are on the precipice of something big. This is the time when they go from being a pre-teen to an actual teenager, if you go by age. Biologically some of these students have already hit puberty, and some have not. I learned this when teaching the novels and short stories that year. Some of the students got the innuendos in the stories, and some did not. You could also tell by looking at some of the boys based on their size, facial hair, and body odor.

Academically, middle school is a hard place to motivate students. They learn very quickly that their grades do not really impact them in terms of college or even moving on to the next grade level. So, the students that do well are the ones that are either self-motivated or have families that have high expectations, a good reward system, and/or the students do not want to disappoint. I was used to being able to motivate my high school students by talking about how it would impact their future, but these students knew their grades did not really impact their future. They knew they would move onto high school regardless of their grades in middle school. Some of them were motivated by the end of the year activities, others not so much. It was eye-opening to say the least. Most of the parents I spoke to were just as frustrated as I was.

My suggestion for those of you with motivation issues in middle school is to work on small goals and small rewards. Work on building self-esteem and positive reinforcement for small changes. Validation is key at this age. Boundaries are essential. This is the time when peers really begin to have an impact both in person and online. Social media should be closely monitored.

High school is an entirely different animal. High school adds a new level of anxiety and stress to teens. Parents and teachers begin to tell their students how much high school impacts their lives. While teachers have been preparing them for this moment their entire academic career, it still is not a reality for most of these students. Remember, these kids are living in the moment. For the freshman, four years is still a long way away. For you parents, it is just around the corner and time is running out. Yet another disconnect is communication. High school is supposed to be the best time of your teen's lives. Many of them have been looking forward to all the social activities that come with high school for a long time: dances, football games, dating, marching band, drama club. Your individual teen has all this in mind. Graduation for a freshman is a long way off.

If you are in the middle of this high school experience with your teen, think about what has been most important to them.

Leonard Sax, in his book *Why Gender Matters*, takes the problem back to kindergarten. He believes that it can be an issue with the fact that we have changed the kindergarten curriculum in a way that does a disservice, especially to boys. Boys aren't necessarily taught to sit and learn how to read and write at the same time as girls. So, forcing a boy to sit and try to learn or separating him into a group that is not learning these concepts, while the girls and some male peers are, makes him very uncomfortable, and he quickly feels stupid. This makes him not want to go to school and dislike learning at an early age that can continue throughout his school years.

Teenagers are at that age where they think they know everything. Adults tend to threaten teenagers with the idea of the real world, but to them the only world that is real is the one they are living in right here, right now. The future real world is a mythical world. They may have an idea of what they want to do in the future, but for most teens this will change a number of times before they decide on an actual career choice. For many of them just getting to graduation is a huge feat.

Adults constantly ask teenagers what they want to do with their lives after high school. The problem comes when parents disagree with the choices their teenagers ultimately make. I have had many students come to see me when they are having a disagreement with their parents about their future college and career choices. It is important to make sure you do not dismiss your teen's future goals outright. This can cause your teen to shut down, rebel, or even get depressed or anxious. I will reinforce here that it is not my goal to tell you how to parent your child, but I have seen what happens when parents do not support their teen's goals. The wedge that it puts between the parents and the teen can often be lifelong. It is your job as a parent to guide your child, to show them all of the options, to explain to them why you believe what you believe, but in the end, unless they are making a decision that will physically or emotionally harm them, you should support them in their decisions. Their decisions may have consequences: they may have to find a job and contribute to the household if they choose not to go to college, for example.

Back when we were in school, there were many more vocational pathways for kids. Not every child was expected to go to college and many, upon leaving high school, had skills that could be used in the workplace. Today, your teen has both more and less choices. Colleges and universities may be harder to get into due to more students applying, but many community colleges are offering students their first two years of education for free.

It is valuable to take the time to act as a guide for your teen, but it is not valuable to create so much stress for both you and your teen that your relationship is strained. Safety and security should always be your goal.

If I were to ask you what a successful high school career looked like for your teen, how would you answer?

An article written by Melissa Fenton on the Grown and Flown website entitled "Trying to be 'Perfect' is Killing Our Teens and We're to Blame" discusses parents putting too much pressure on their teens. Fenton gives statistics from the CDC showing the record numbers of teens with feelings of anxiety and depression:

- "More than one in three high school students had experienced persistent feelings of sadness or hopelessness in 2019, a 40 percent increase since 2009."
- "In 2019, approximately one in six youths reported making a suicide plan in the past year, a 44 percent increase since 2009."

Fenton also discusses both the CDC's views and her own beliefs as to why, "stumped researchers, social scientists, and psychologists have only begun to investigate the causes, many of which they have linked to smart phone and social media use, but is that really it? It could be, seeing as how they're growing up under a selfie spotlight—with images of perfection constantly loading in their devices—perpetuating the great lie that everyone else has it more together and better than they do."

Retired Tennessee teacher, former colleague, and friend Charmaine Briggs sent me her story to share in response to this idea of perfection and how it impacted her as a young teacher,

"As a teacher, I learned the hard way that comparison is indeed the thief of joy. I wonder how hard it hits teens who don't have the emotional maturity to manage those feelings. Perfection is elusive to most and sought after by many. Teenagers these days are fighting internal battles that are only exacerbated by social media images of false perfection. Students with or without cords at graduation have fought battles that their parents may or may not have been aware of. Why are they not talking to their parents? They may be talking to their teachers, as you well know. Whether they are striving for better appearance, better friends, or better grades, their battle is every day. It just seems to be tougher these days.

Thirty years ago when I started out as a new teacher, I was introduced to a student's battle within the first six weeks of school. Only I was ill-equipped to see the signs. I was helpless to help the child who yelled in my face one day, "Mrs. Briggs, you just don't understand me!" I took his antics (an accidental eraser thrown in my face) and disrespect in class as an affront. I did not take the time to have a conversation with him to understand him. Then he was suddenly absent from school. Two weeks after his outburst in my classroom, thirteen-year-old CW took his own life at the end of a shotgun in his rural Virginia home. It was an awakening, a sad and preventable loss—not because I did not intervene, but because of all the adults in his life who did not intervene. That first-year lesson guided me in developing positive relationships with my students for the remainder of my career."

While Mrs. Briggs's story had a tragic ending, so many of our teens feel this need to be perfect. They compare themselves to their peers, or the version of their peers they see online every day and many of them find themselves lacking. They look at the expectations they place on themselves or the ones you, their parents, place on them and feel that they cannot meet them (even when this is totally untrue). So, they turn inward or they lash out, and the adults in their lives have to be vigilant.

While this story is so very tragic, the reality is your teens are feeling the pressure. This is true no matter whether they show it or not. Some feel like they cannot do anything right, so why bother trying, some feel that if they cannot do it right, they shouldn't try, some feel like if they cannot get it perfect their world is ending. There are some laid back kids who take things in stride, but they are definitely in the minority. This happens in many aspects of their lives not just school.

Have you ever said to your child who received a B on a test or an assignment, "Why didn't you get an A?" or even to your child who received an A-, "Why wasn't it an A?" This so undermines their self-esteem. Many times, they tried their best. They were so proud of their accomplishment, they couldn't wait to tell you, and it still wasn't good enough.

Or your child who maybe usually fails a math test comes home with a passing grade, and you say something like, "you can do better." There goes their motivation to try the next time and their anxiety goes up.

The student with straight As but one missing assignment gets berated by his parents for not doing that assignment without being given credit and compliments for all his hard work.

Think about how you feel at work when your accomplishments go unnoticed or even at home when you don't get noticed for the things you do well.

Anxiety and motivation are so often tied together.

What Can You Do as a Parent?

- Be aware of your own anxiety when dealing with your teens. They are aware of it, and it changes the way they interact with you.
- Be aware of the amount of anxiety you are projecting onto your teens by pressuring them to be perfect. They don't have to be perfect. Perfection is an illusion.
- Motivate your teens where they are at. Keep the bar high but utilize their wants and desires.

CHAPTER 9

WHY TEENS NEED TRUSTED ADULTS

———

Five-year-old Lisa sat on the floor and waited not so patiently for the end of the *Romper Room* episode as she did every time she watched it. She couldn't wait for all the other children to be sitting just like she was crisscross applesauce on the floor waiting for the teacher to say the magic words, "Romper, bomper, stomper, boo, tell me, tell me, tell me do. Magic Mirror, tell me today, did all my friends have fun at play?" Because then she would look through the magic mirror and call out the names of the children she saw that day. "I see, Tina and John and Katherine and Ryan and…" Every day, Lisa would wait for the teacher to see her, and on the special days when her name would be called, she would fill with joy that she was seen. It didn't happen often, but those days were the best.

I don't remember much about the show *Romper Room* itself, but the teacher calling out those names while looking through that magic mirror has stuck with me my whole life. It's the first memory I have of truly being seen, and it wasn't even real, but boy did it feel real. No matter how old we are, we want to be seen. Teens in particular, even when hiding in their rooms, want to be seen. They want to be understood. Sometimes, this understanding can only come, from their vantage point, from someone other than you, the parent.

Young children look up to their parents. They also look up to most authority figures in their lives, and those that show them special attention. As time goes on, children unfortunately learn that not all adults can be trusted. Sometimes they become wary of trusting any adult, other times they gravitate towards trusted adults out of necessity, and some, like me, are lucky enough to have many trusted adults in their lives to turn to.

Think back to your teenage years. Did you have an adult, or more than one adult, in your life who you turned to when life got out of hand? Someone you turned to when you needed advice? Or just a friendly ear? Who was that adult that you trusted? For some maybe it was a parent or other family member, for others it was a teacher, coach, youth leader, pastor, scout or troop leader. No matter who it was, they may still be a part of your life or maybe you just have fond recollections of the impact they had on you. Hopefully, you let them know what they meant to you because I can tell you from experience that there is nothing more rewarding than knowing I made an impact on my students' lives.

While it might be painful for your teens to no longer be turning to you for all the answers, this is the time in their lives when this will happen. Brooklyn Rainey sums it up nicely in her book *One Trusted Adult*, "The job of the parent is to surround the child with people like you: adults who have strong values and the child's best interest in mind. Professionals who know how to build trust with young people while maintaining healthy and clear boundaries."

Mentors play many different roles in the lives of teens. You may in fact be one of your teen's mentors, but teens will also need other trusted adults to turn to at times in their lives. This should not make you feel like less of a parent or feel left out. These other adults are there to provide support and guidance for your teen at a time when they are seeking their independence from you. This is a good thing. Remember, this is the period in their life where they are transitioning from being a child to an adult. They are learning the tools they need to be able to eventually go out on their own. They are on their own hero's journey like many of the characters they have seen in the books they have read, the movies they have watched, the games they have played. On this journey, every hero has their own mentor that helps them reach their destination: their dream. In my interview with Emmy-winning author and motivational speaker Clint Pulver, he reminded me, "Luke Skywalker had Obi Wan Kenobi, Frodo had Gandalf, Katniss Everdeen had Haymitch, Aladdin had the genie."

What makes a mentor a truly significant person in another's life was summed up nicely by Pulver. In our interview, he had five Cs of mentorship he shared with me. These make so much sense, especially when talking about mentoring teens. They apply whether you are a parent, teacher, coach, or anyone else involved in mentoring young people. These characteristics should resonate with you.

The five Cs:

1. Confidence
2. Credibility
3. Competence
4. Candor
5. The ability to *care* for the people that they serve

You cannot just be handed the title of mentor. Another point Pulver stresses: true mentors are advocates. They not only help develop you, but they also advocate for you and are the catalyst for helping make your dreams happen.

John Link was this type of mentor for me. When I was a student athletic trainer, the training room was attached to the athletic director's office. John was one of the assistant athletic directors when I started high school, so I was with him an awful lot. We got to know each other. He became a sounding board for me about a lot of things. Life, academics, my newfound love of athletic training. He was also a bit of a protector for me, as the boys locker room was also attached to the training room, and teenage boys will be teenage boys with crude remarks that made me laugh but made Coach Link become Papa Bear when he deemed it necessary. Those boys were made to apologize a number of times, which made me feel about ten feet tall. John also introduced me to the athletic trainer at California State University, Fullerton to do an observation in their training room. This helped solidify my desire to continue to become a certified athletic trainer. This led to her writing a letter of recommendation for me for acceptance into UCLA's athletic training program, which I attended. John also showed me how much respect adults can have for teens, and that they can learn as much from us as we can learn from them. John was not afraid to ask for help when it came to technology. I taught him a lot about how to use the new technology in his office. He was very appreciative and told me often. His validation of my skills helped boost my confidence. His mentorship continued after I graduated from high school and up until his death. He was instrumental in my being hired as both a teacher and an athletic trainer, and I turned to him on a regular basis for support and guidance.

Keith Hawkins became a motivational speaker because at age fifteen he saw a motivational speaker who validated him. As I have previously discussed, validation for teens is so important, and when this validation occurred, Teenage Keith was able to open his mind and his heart to the message he heard, which was "change doesn't happen unless it starts with me. If I want people to treat me better, I have to treat people better, and if I want people to not stereotype me, I have to stop stereotyping people." Ironically, he had been stereotyping this speaker. The speaker was a white guy on a basketball court. Young Keith was looking at him thinking, "this guy can't play basketball," but it turned out he could, and the speaker used that to show him that you don't want people judging you like you just judged me, and it resonated with Keith enough that now as an adult he is speaking to teens himself.

Being there for these teens and having candid conversations with them is something that many mentors offer your teens.

A former student named Monica told me her math teacher in high school, "constantly reminded me that I need to say 'no' sometimes. I don't have to do everything people ask of me. He is also the one who told me I should be a teacher and not a psychologist. He never forced his thoughts on me. He would just make comments and let me sit on them. He would get me to teach other students, whether during class or tutoring. We had a lot of honest conversations that got me thinking about what I wanted, rather than what I believe others wanted of me."

When the situation is about home, teens need a place to turn. These trusted adults offer a safe place to vent without judgment and can often offer sound advice and even diffuse the situation.

It was Holly's basketball coach who gave her a safe place to break down. "Sometime before I was diagnosed with my mental illnesses, my basketball coach saw me crouching outside my classroom and asked me what was wrong. For some unknown reason, people asking me that just makes things worse, and I just ended up having a full breakdown in front of him. He took me to his classroom, and we just talked about things. He told me I should talk to my mom, and that if I felt I couldn't do it, that he'd help me. Coach has kids of his own, and because my own father is not around much, I guess I see him as a father figure. Especially because he takes breakdowns in stride. He just makes me feel safe and is constantly assuring me that he and his wife are always there for me."

Amber turned to her aunt because she listened and also challenged her about her feelings. "I was having a lot of trouble at home and I didn't quite know what to do about the situation or even how to feel, so I decided to meet with her and ask for advice and just vent about the situation."

There's so much truth in what Clint Pulver said, "There's a lot of leaders… or coaches or even parents that can command fear, or they can get results. But does it last?" The fear lasts and we might remember that we were afraid of this person, even that we were willing to do anything not to incur their wrath, but there has to be more than that for them to be a mentor.

Many of my students would tell me that when they first got to my class, they were afraid of me. They told me they had heard my class was hard, and I made my students work. If you asked most of the students who were in my class they would agree they had worked hard, but I was not mean or evil. They did not want to disappoint me because they knew

I wanted them to be successful and had their best interests at heart. I was not working them just for the sake of working them. The ones that took the time to get to know me found out how truly invested in them I was.

I was introduced to Clint Pulver's story during one of my faculty meetings. At the end of the meeting, our administrators played a video entitled *Be a Mr. Jensen* that told the story of Clint and his teacher, Mr. Jensen. Recently, Clint won an Emmy for a version of this same story entitled, *You're Not a Problem, You're an Opportunity.* This story is about Clint at ten-years-old. He would fidget in class and was constantly getting in trouble for it. One day Mr. Jensen asked him to stay after class. He thought he was in trouble again, but Mr. Jensen assured him he wasn't. After class, he took young Clint aside and asked him if he ever thought about playing the drums.

Clint Pulver emphasized to me in our interview that the focus must be on connection and emphasizing what matters most to the person with whom you are trying to connect.

Great mentors get to the part about the mentee. So, every kid is asking a parent "let me know when it gets to the part about me." And a lot of people hear that, and they go "well those entitled little shining stars in my life"… and I would say it's not so much about entitlement as it is about good parenting, about bringing humanity back into the house, the classroom, the workplace. Because everybody wants to be seen, everybody wants to be heard, and everybody wants to be understood. And I think sometimes you know there is that aspect of I'm the parent. I'm the parent, you are the child. But again, there is no significant loyalty, without significant connection. I do believe that, like

there's no significant learning happens in the classroom without significant connection… So the point
is to connect. Connect, and see what matters to them.

This really resonates with me, as I hope it will with you. As
children and teenagers, this idea of wanting it to be about
them is not all about being selfish. They are starving for connection. They will make it in any way they can, and sometimes that leads them down the path of making bad choices
if they do not have good role models, good mentors because
they will take whatever connections they can get.

Clint Pulver says that Mr. Jensen did two things for him
in his life. "He was the person that communicated my potential. And he communicated my worth. And he did it so well
to the point that I saw it within myself. He got to the part
about me, and everybody else saw the limitation, everybody
else tried to develop me, everybody tried to fix me. And he
was the person that decided to connect, and he did it in a
way that created a moment."

It's those moments that are the difference that make the
difference. When Mr. Jensen handed Clint Pulver those
drumsticks and told him he was not a problem but a drummer, he changed the way Clint saw himself. He gave Clint
worth. He went beyond the literal noise that Clint had been
making in class and saw Clint for who he was to become. He
connected to a dream that Clint didn't even know existed, but
his body had been speaking for him, and Mr. Jensen listened
to his body language and saw a drummer not a noise maker.

"And from that moment on, my behavior changed. I
participated more in class. I raised my hand more. I
was more quiet. I focused on trying not to move as

much because of what he did, he was on my team. He became the advocate, not just the developer, not just the teacher. He truly became somebody that I knew cared about me and cared about what mattered to me. And in doing so that changed my behavior, and it built loyalty, it built engagement."

It built a lifetime connection. Clint told me during our interview that he had just had Mr. Jensen over to his house for dinner three nights before our interview. He was a part of his family. That's the power of those types of moments, those types of relationships.

In my own life, I had that same type of relationship with my mentor Mark Takkinen before he passed. I still have that type of relationship with some of my other mentors.

We still get together for lunch. I still tell them on a regular basis what they mean to me. They are invited to major milestone events.

One such mentor is Marjie Blevins. She is my teaching inspiration, and she was my sophomore English teacher. She looked at me when I was fifteen years old and told me I was going to be an English teacher. I was a math and science kid at the time and laughed at her because of course I was a teenager, and I knew better, and there was no way I was going to become an English teacher. I loved English, but math and science were my jam. When I came back to student teach, she laughed so hard she snorted because she had known all along. Marjie was and is the type of teacher who cares so much about her students that she carries that with her always. She wants the best for, and of, her students at all times. She expends every ounce of herself on her students every day, and her passion for teaching and her students shines in everything she does. I tell her all the time if that I expended the amount of energy she does in one class period during my whole day, I would be exhausted. She's the type of teacher that dresses up as Scout when she teaches *To Kill a Mockingbird.* She makes her students crawl on the floor, and gets on the floor and crawls with them, when she's teaching "The Yellow Wallpaper." She also brought in her own mentor John Wayne "Jack" Schlatter, who also wrote for *Chicken Soup for the Soul,* for twenty-nine years before he passed to motivate her students and share his wisdom and kindness with them, so they would be touched by his stories and compassion just as she had been. Over the years, I have shared Jack's stories with my students. My best friend Heather, who also had Marjie as a teacher, typically reads Jack's book *Gifts by the Side of the Road* to her students every year, showing the generational impact mentors can have.

Keith Hawkins said his mentors taught him some valuable life lessons: Miss Clark taught him that his preconceived thoughts that he wasn't smart enough were incorrect and that thoughts and actions were connected. "You think so poorly of yourself, if you change the way you think it will change what you do." Mr. Estrada and others taught him not to be so fearful. He believes a lot of that fear is taught at home. He was taught to fear that people were using him, and these teachers helped him unlearn that. Instead, there are people who really want a good future for you.

My parents were mentors to many of my friends growing up. My mom did not realize the impact she had on their lives until much later. Some of these relationships were more direct: my parents took in one of my friends for a couple of months when she left her house because of a bad situation at home. But more than that, they made my friends feel welcome and like our house was their house too. For some of them it was a home away from home. For some of them it was just another place they could hang out and/or call home, and for others it was more of a home than their own could ever be.

My parents were not intrusive. Most of the time you wouldn't even know they were there. Except my mom might be in the kitchen cooking up hot dogs or spaghetti to feed the hungry horde or chatting with one or another of us while she was helping my grandmother. If we were having a party for a birthday or one of the major holidays, my parents would be mingling. My dad would be telling jokes or offering words of advice. Sometimes my friends would show up and instead of saying, "Hi, Lisa," they would say, "Where are your parents?" This went on until they sold the house. The first holiday after my parents sold the house my friends and I mourned its loss.

My mom doesn't feel like she did anything special, but her presence as a trusted adult who would have candid conversations with teenagers was super important. I was lucky. I had other parents in my friend's group who were like this as well. We had several homes we could go to and feel like we could turn to the adults.

Don't feel bad if your teen doesn't want to hang out at your house. Some teens don't want their space invaded, and it has nothing to do with you as a parent. This is just one example.

Parents are mentors as well. Both of my parents have been mentors to me in different ways. My mother has been my best friend for most of my life. I knew I could ask her almost any question, and she would give me an honest answer. My father is not only the man I tried to emulate for success, but also the person I never wanted to disappoint. When I was young, I used to love going car shopping with him. He is a master negotiator, and I would sit and watch him go back and forth with the car salesman, making phone calls to other dealerships, making the salesman sweat, wondering if he would get the sale. When we left with the car, I felt what I realized later was pride, knowing my dad always had the best deal. I even had friends who took my dad with them to buy cars. When I went to work for him in college, I felt the same sense of pride watching him in meetings. It fortified my own work ethic as a teacher.

Your children look up to you. Many of them already think of you as mentors. When I surveyed my students about who their current mentors are, most of them said one of their parents. They still feel you are the person they will turn to if they need something, or they want to.

It's all about the moments. In my interview with Clint, I asked him how adults can have a positive influence on teenagers. It all came back to this idea of connection and moments. He shared a couple of stories that really show why this is important to teenagers:

One was about a boy and his father. "I'll never forget; I was speaking to a bunch of kids and this kid came up and he showed me a post of him and his football team. And he said, 'look at this, look at this picture' and we were talking about the football team. And he said, 'check the site, *my dad liked my post. It is crazy, right?*' I'm like, no big deal, but to the kid, it mattered. Social media matters in a lot of people's lives. The boy just cared about the simple fact that his dad took the time to like his post.

The second story was about a mother who was a marathon runner who was so into fitness that she was constantly pushing fitness and diets and health on her daughter, but her daughter loved drama. The daughter told Clint, "the best thing ever was [when] my mom got me tickets to go to my favorite show."

By getting these tickets, this mother showed she understood what mattered to her daughter. Clint Pulver emphasized in our interview that moments like the one with the father liking his son's social media posts and the mother buying the play tickets, "it's those little moments where what matters to you matters to me. And then when you advocate to help them to remember that you actually remember what matters to them."

Keith Hawkins talks about one of the most important things you have to offer your teen: Time. Parents work so hard at trying to make a better life for their kids they often forget that the one thing their children really want is more of them. He reflected on his own relationship with his mother and says, "the reason why the relationship wasn't as good as it could have been was because she didn't spend the time and most parents don't. A parent doing great for their kids is providing. So, we spend a lot of time providing when we come home and we're tired. That's why one of my quotes is, 'find a way out of no way.' It's like there's no way I have energy for my kids, there's no way I have energy to go through this and that. But you've got to find it because they might forget the things that you say, but they never forget the things that you do with them. I would say time is the most important thing when it comes to kids. Find time to hang out with your kids, and I'm not saying so much to be their best friend, but I think if you spend time with them, you will become one of those best friends, for your time is important."

One of the assignments I gave my students recently was to watch a movie with their parents that was from the decade that their parents were in high school, so that they could all relate to and discuss how it related to their own high school experience. One of my students submitted a response to the movie *Back to the Future*. The student said that his mom had compared Doc Brown to "that one teacher, the one that cares and takes the time to teach you but also cares about you and your well-being. The teacher that makes you feel like anything is possible, the one that motivates you to do your best." This mother called those teachers her "Docs." I reached out to this mother and explained that I was writing this book and asked her if she would be willing to tell me about one of her Docs. Ironically, when she sat down and really thought about the one person she would write about as her Doc she didn't choose a teacher. She chose her mother. Below is the response I received from her.

> *My 'Doc' would have to be my mom, I know it might sound like a cliché but she really is my Doc. However, I didn't always know or realize how much she really means to me and how much she has helped me until I got older.*
>
> *Growing up all I saw was two parents who left me alone with my brothers to look after and care for and it made me mad. The reality of it all was that my dad would work as many hours as he was allowed to work and get paid less than minimum wage because he was an immigrant and would be threatened by his boss on a daily basis. My mom would leave the house early in the morning to catch the bus to clean houses and then she would go to the church to get a box of food with*

fruits and vegetables that looked spoiled and canned food without labels so it was always a surprise to open those up. My mom had a way to make food last and feed all of us on a budget. It amazes me how we never starved because of my mom's creative dishes. You'd be surprised how many ways we can eat beans and rice and still have each bite taste so delicious that you don't tire of it. Little did I know that everything I complained about would help me out in life and make me the independent and confident individual that I am today.

I had a lot of responsibilities at a very young age; being the only girl and the oldest of six children, it all fell on me. I remember making rice, sopitas and weenies and eggs for my brothers at the age of five. I know it might seem unreal because nowadays five-year-olds are not allowed near the stove but it's true. I remember changing diapers and washing cloth diapers at a very young age. I had many responsibilities and not a lot of freedom. I was not able to go out or participate in any after-school activities. My parents would always leave me with my brothers to look after and cook and clean. By the time my mom got home dinner was made, the house was clean, and my brothers were fed or doing homework. I did it all, I was like a mother to my brothers.

My mother worked from early morning until… well, I'm not sure. I don't know when she slept. I always saw her doing stuff. Looking for work, teaching herself to drive, going to school to learn English, helping out my grandmother and saving every penny to be able to buy our first home and our second home. My mom has an inner strength that always, till this day, keeps her going *regardless of what others say or think of her. My mom dresses how she feels comfortable, speaks her mind and is super kind and friendly. She seems to always know someone everywhere we go and makes new friends at any given time or place. The words 'can't' and 'no' do not exist in her vocabulary and if anyone tells her that she can't or no she takes it on as a challenge and proves them wrong. My mother is very wise and lived a tough childhood, never knowing her father as she was a result of a rape and seeing her own mother struggle for survival. Escaping a kidnap and escaping a terrible situation of almost being sexually abused by her own uncle. My mother has been through a lot and yet none of those horrible experiences 'broke' her soul, or her being. She is a wonderful mother and a true friend, and I am honored to be her daughter.*

Having all the responsibilities that I had at such a young age and missing out on school events did not prevent me from experiencing life. It prepared me for a world filled with obstacles. The love of my parents and brothers has been more than I ever hoped for, they are here till this day for me and my kids. Everything I know and am is all credited to my mom, whom without her guidance and love I would not be here today.

This is the response of an adult woman reflecting back on her mother as a mother herself. She shows the resentment she had as a child and the things she had to sacrifice. She recognizes that as a child she did not always understand what was happening, but as an adult she sees through enlightened eyes. I told her that if she hadn't shared this with her mother, she should. We don't always let our parents know that we have this understanding of all they have sacrificed for their children. This mother even thanked me for assigning this project because the whole family sat down and watched this movie together and discussed the film and the things in the film that the children didn't know about. The son mentioned in his assignment that he did not know what a Walkman or a cassette player was, and he was amazed at how far technology has come. Little things like this can help bridge the gap between parents and their children.

What You Can Do as a Parent?

- Encourage your teen's relationships with other trusted adults.
- Don't take it personally when they don't come to you for everything.
- Be a mentor to others when possible.
- Give your teen your time.

CONCLUSION

———

Sixteen-year-old Lisa walked into the kitchen and saw that her mom was on the phone. She needed to ask her if she could go to Heather's house. She sat at the kitchen table drumming her fingers impatiently on the countertop.

"So, I need to pick up Jason at school after soccer practice, then Harvey wants me to make dinner, so I have to go to the grocery store."

After about a minute of listening to this boring conversation, Lisa decided this conversation was taking too long. She walked over to where her mom was talking on the phone and poked her.

"Mom."

Her mom put one finger in the air, telling her to wait a minute.

Lisa rolled her eyes. She didn't want to wait a minute. She poked her again.

"Mom."

Her mom tried to walk away. Lisa followed and poked her again.

"Mom."

Her mom whirled on her. Hand over the receiver and yelled, "What?"

"Can I go to Heather's?"

"Fine. Just go away."

Lisa trotted off happily.

Lisa's mom turned back to her conversation, "Why is it that when I'm not on the phone they don't need anything, but the minute I get on the phone, they are right here poking me, needing something?"

Sound familiar? This was probably something we did to my poor mother more often than I'd like to admit. She hated the poking. Sometimes we'd just keep poking her until she relented. Now we could've just texted her and asked, but back in the day, she was tethered to the wall, and could only escape if she hung up on the person she was talking to or put the phone down and literally fled.

Being the parent of a teenager is terrifying and rewarding all at the same time. Your baby is getting closer to the time when they are going to spread their wings and become an adult. The last thing you want is for them to stop communicating with you.

In order for that communication to flourish and be more productive, a balancing act must ensue. Your emotions must be tamped down, while your teenagers are in this heightened state. As you have seen in this book, this is not easy, but it is worth it.

The teenage brain is in flux. It is working hard to form into a well-oiled machine that will work well for them during their adult years, but it is not ready to be left entirely on its own. The resistance to this is inevitable, but there are ways to mitigate this resistance if you are willing to do the work with patience and, most importantly, love. Love should be easy.

You wouldn't have picked up this book in the first place if you didn't love your teen. You may struggle with liking their words and actions at times, but you do love them.

Take a deep breath. Remember, you are the parent. They are the child. No matter what, you do get to make the decisions about their safety. The more you can communicate with them that your decisions are truly about their safety, the more likely they are to understand where you are coming from.

Making these decisions about their safety is not always easy. Social media, video games, the internet have all made this more difficult as you navigate the "when's" and the "how's" of it all but know that setting and communicating clear boundaries helps.

Mentors help too.

As a teen I had so many adults that helped shape me into the person I am today. My parents for sure, but I also was lucky enough to have a plethora of teachers and coaches who impacted my life. As I reflect back on how these people entered my life, I know that some of them I initiated the relationships with, but for the most part, it was the way that they interacted with me that made all the difference. Your own teens may have mentors already, if not guide them to find mentors outside of your household. They need trusted adults who they can confide in, look up to, and get their confidence boosts from.

I'll share one more mentor story.

The first time I met Robin Oliver as a teacher she was standing on the lab table in front of her classroom. She had her hair in a severe bun and wore a lab coat. From the top of this lab table, she scared the living daylights out of the twenty-five or so freshmen sitting in her ninth-grade biology class. I wasn't sure about this woman. For one, she had me collecting bugs over the summer (even while I was in Hawaii) for a dreaded insect project that I had heard about going into high school and for another, I now thought of her as this crazy lady who was going to be mean to us for all of freshman year. The next day she came in a totally different woman, telling us how much fun biology was going to be, and it turned out to be one of my favorite classes that year (except for that insect collection. I still hate bugs of all kinds). Robin was also the International Baccalaureate (IB) coordinator, and I was an IB candidate, so she was one of my advisors throughout high school. I worked with her on my IB extended essay (a research-based essay that had to be completed my senior year). She advised me on college, listened when I need it, met my family, and we became colleagues and friends when I came to work at the same high school I attended. Robin and I are still friends to this day, and she had a huge impact on my life. Robin's impact came from her willingness to listen and her encouragement. This has continued throughout my life.

What I want you to see about the people who I chose as mentors or who chose to mentor me (I'm still not sure which) is the impact that had on my life beyond my teenage years. Whether I still see or talk to them or not, the resonance in my life is almost palpable.

I became a teacher in part because of the influence these people had on my life as a teenager. I wanted to have that same influence on the life of other teens. Your teenagers need mentors who can guide them.

My parents were also a huge guiding force in my life. I had different relationships with each of them, but we were a family first. My mom and I could talk about almost anything. My dad and I actually became closer during my teen years, but our relationship continued to grow the older I got. It wasn't that I didn't feel I could talk to him; I could, and I did talk to him about a lot of things, but he was the person I looked up to the most and wanted to make proud. The strongest memories both my brother and I have are of family vacations growing up.

Communication, both verbal and non-verbal, is in every interaction you have with your teen. They are watching you; you are watching them. Make the most of each of these encounters.

Put yourself in their shoes. Not as the teenager you once were, but as the teenager they now are. They may be a mini version of you. You may often say, they are just like I was at that age, but they are not you. Their experiences are different from yours. Learn from the mistakes of the past, but don't let them create so much fear that your relationships suffer.

On a positive note, remember you are not in this alone. Every parent who has ever had to deal with a teenager has gone through some of what you are going through. It will be very reassuring to know others have been through this. Talk to them. Ask them about their experiences. Their stories will help you understand your teen is normal, in some cases even better than you thought.

You've got this!

ACKNOWLEDGMENTS

———

First, I have to thank my parents for supporting me unconditionally in this endeavor, and mom specifically for giving me feedback on the book even when she was afraid of what she might find out about herself as a parent.

I am grateful for my brother Jason who always made me glad to be able to say we fought but not like other siblings.

Thank you to my grandmother, Sydelle, may she rest in peace, who taught every one of us Jass's the importance of family, and to the rest of the Jass family who are all connected to this crazy mishpucha, thank you for always being there for me.

Next, I'd like to thank all of the mentors named specifically in this book: Mark Takkinen, John Link, Robin Oliver, and Marjie Blevins. I'd also like to thank those who had an impact on me both as a child and an adult whose stories did not make it to the pages of this book. You all made me the woman I am today, and I am obsessively grateful to each of you.

I had the pleasure to personally interview some amazing people for this book. They were chosen for the impact their work has had on me personally and on the lives of others, most notably teens:

Jon Gordon's books have been part of my personal development journey for a long time. The first book I read of his was *The Energy Bus*, and it helped change the way I interacted with people in different aspects of my life by not allowing them to be energy vampires. I have several of his quotes hanging in my classroom, and I use many of his positivity tools in my instruction. Thank you, Jon for your impact on my life!

I have had the pleasure of hearing Keith Hawkins speak to my students at Bellflower High School for the past couple of years. His passion for connecting with teens inspires me. Thank you, Keith!

Clint Pulver uses his own story to inspire both teachers and kids alike. His story reminds me to look beneath the surface and figure out what makes each kid tick on an individual level. Thank you, Clint!

I'd also like to thank my 2020-2021 classes at Bellflower High School. My senior students in periods two, four, and six, and my freshmen students in period five. Your willingness to share your personal stories with me and give your candid insight into the mind of today's teenager helped give this book its heart.

To all the students I taught at Sonora High School, Ravenwood High School, Centennial High School, and Bellflower High School who see yourself in this book both in specific stories or feel represented in these pages. Thank you for making an impact on me. Being a part of your lives makes me want to be a better teacher and a better person every day.

Thank you, Niurka, for guiding me to open my eyes, my heart, my mind, and my ears during my own transformational journey to allow me to see more clearly the path to my life's work.

To all the people who supported this book before it was available, thank you for helping make my dreams a reality. It means more to me than you could ever know:

Michele Jass-Houghton, Robin Oliver, Marjorie Blevins, Harvey and Pat Jass, Jalena Mietzner, Shelly Straim, Heather Bradley, Gina Frazier, Lynne Yost, Steven Jass, Elizabeth Eden, Albert Lopez, Ronae Wilkes, Brady Bove, Carolyn Brown, Pam Colletti, Veronica Reynolds, Sharon Freilich, Rebecca Sullivan, Candy Woolf, Mark Smuts, Kelly Kelly, Ted and Linda Jass, Lisa Guttmann, Ruth Vadnais, Alice Mack, Sheryl Bender, Erin Thurmond, Gary Hunt, Pamela Fossler, Aaron Dacuycuy, Khadijah Dibia, Jessica Jenkins, Christine Clarke, William Hiser, Jamie Despot-Sissom, Jenny Wesson, Wendy Watt, David and April Haller, Kim Brooks, Jeff Owen, Esther Amsterdam, Rich and Cherilyn Lodding, Joseph Ames and Amy Crofoot, Jennifer Smith, Danielle Scipio, Michael Hunter, David Kaz, Melissa Ellis, Zuleyma Denise Rodriguez, Adam Smith, Jennifer Ailstock, Krystal Fierro-Garcia, Emily Silva, Shanon Resco, Charmaine Briggs, Ellen Frasier, Emilie Totten, Amy Wright, Jennie McElroy, Kristine Acosta, Carol Skowronski, Quincy Francis, Joelle Edmunds, Elizabeth Dunkerson, Cassandra Agnew, Rebecca Schwartz, Georgia Bratton Taylor, Drew Paige, Ann Morgeson, Jeanne Link, Ron Jass, Faith Beall, Sarah Gibson, Mark and Jo Jass, Patrick, Deann and Cody Takkinen, Gabriela Bermudez, Eric Koester, Terri Nakamura, Terry Grossgold, Kara Biagiotti.

Finally, a huge thank you to the New Degree Press, especially Eric Koester, Brian Bies, and Kathy Wood, for helping make the book of my heart a reality.

APPENDIX

———

Introduction

American Psychological Association. "Mental Health Issues Increased Significantly in Young Adults over Last Decade: Shift May Be Due in Part to Rise of Digital Media, Study Suggests." *ScienceDaily*, March 15, 2019. https://www.sciencedaily.com/releases/2019/03/190315110908.htm.

Chapter 1

Blakemore, Sarah-Jayne. *Inventing Ourselves: The Secret Life of the Teenage Brain*. New York: PublicAffairs, 2018.

Dobbs, David. "Beautiful Brains." *National Geographic*. October 1, 2011. https://www.nationalgeographic.com/magazine/article/beautiful-brains.

Dobbs, David, B. J. Casey, and Dr. Jay Giedd. "Understanding the Mysterious Teenage Brain." Radio Show. NPR. September 20, 2011. https://www.npr.org/2011/09/20/140637115/understanding-the-mysterious-teenage-brain.

Elkind, David. "Egocentrism in Adolescence." *Child Development* 38, no. 4 (1967): 1025-034. Accessed May 11, 2021. doi:10.2307/1127100.

Ginsburg, Kenneth. "Treasuring Our Teens with Dr. Ken Ginsburg." Interview by Liz Gumbinner. *Spawned Parenting.* Apple Podcasts. March 18, 2019. Audio. 35:14. https://podcasts.apple.com/kg/podcast/spawned-parenting-podcast-kristen-liz-coolmompicks/id1002671438?i=1000432202724.

Jensen, Frances E. *The Teenage Brain: A Neuroscientist's Survival Guide to Raising Adolescents and Young Adults.* New York, NY: Harper, 2016.

Scott, Maiken. "When the Imaginary Audience Becomes More Real." *The Pulse.* WHYY. 10:04. May 26, 2016. https://whyy.org/segments/when-the-imaginary-audience-becomes-more-real/.

Chapter 2

American Academy of Child and Adolescent Psychiatry. "Social Media and Teens." Aacap.org. Updated March 2018. https://www.aacap.org/AACAP/Families_and_Youth/Facts_for_Families/FFF-Guide/Social-Media-and-Teens-100.aspx.

Anderson, Monica, and Jingjing Jiang. "Teens, Social Media & Technology 2018." Pew Research Center: Internet, Science & Tech. Pew Research Center. May 31, 2018. https://www.pewresearch.org/internet/2018/05/31/teens-social-media-technology-2018/.

Lenhart, Amanda. "Teens, Social Media & Technology Overview 2015." Pew Research Center: Internet, Science & Tech. Pew Research Center. April 9, 2015. https://www.pewresearch.org/internet/2015/04/09/teens-social-media-technology-2015/.

Natterson, Cara. *Decoding Boys: New Science behind the Subtle Art of Raising Sons.* New York: Ballantine, 2021.

Pew Research Center. "Anxiety and Depression Top List of Problems Teens See among Their Peers." Pew Research Center's Social & Demographic Trends Project. Pew Research Center, February 14, 2019. https://www.pewresearch.org/social-trends/2019/02/20/most-u-s-teens-see-anxiety-and-depression-as-a-major-problem-among-their-peers/psdt_02-20-19_teens-00-00/.

Orlowski, Jeff, dir. *The Social Dilemma.* Netflix, 2020. https://www.netflix.com/title/81254224.

Chapter 3

Ginsberg, Kenneth. "Treasuring Our Teens with Dr. Ken Ginsburg." Interview by Liz Gumbinner. *Spawned Parenting.* Apple Podcasts. March 18, 2019. Audio. 35:14. https://podcasts.apple.com/kg/podcast/spawned-parenting-podcast-kristen-liz-coolmom-picks/id1002671438?i=1000432202724.

Gordon, Jon. *The Positive Dog: A Story about the Power of Positivity.* Hoboken, N. J.: John Wiley, 2012.

Rainey, Brooklyn. *One Trusted Adult: How to Build Strong Connections & Healthy Boundaries with Young People.* USA: Circle Talk, 2019. Kindle.

Shipp, Josh. *The Grown-Up's Guide to Teenage Humans: How to Decode Their Behavior, Develop Trust, and Raise a Respectable Adult.* New York: Harper Wave, 2018. Kindle.

Chapter 4

Ginsberg, Kenneth. "Treasuring Our Teens with Dr. Ken Ginsburg." Interview by Liz Gumbinner. *Spawned Parenting.* Apple Pod-

casts. March 18, 2019. Audio. 35:14. https://podcasts.apple.com/
kg/podcast/spawned-parenting-podcast-kristen-liz-coolmom-
picks/id1002671438?i=1000432202724.

Tarantino, Quentin, dir. *Pulp Fiction.* 1994. IMDb. 2021.
https://www.imdb.com/title/tt0110912/characters/nm0000235.

Rainey, Brooklyn. *One Trusted Adult: How to Build Strong Connections & Healthy Boundaries with Young People.* USA: Circle
Talk, 2019. Kindle.

Chapter 5

Bialik, Mayim. *Boying Up: How to Be Brave, Bold and Brilliant.*
New York, NY: Penguin Books, 2019.

Bialik, Mayim. *Girling Up: How to Be Strong, Smart and Spectac-
ular.* New York, NY: Penguin Books, 2019.

Hadlee, Celeste. "10 Ways to Have a Better Conversation." Filmed May
2015 in Savannah, GA. TED video, 11:21. https://www.ted.com/
talks/celeste_headlee_10_ways_to_have_a_better_conversation.

Chapter 6

Barbor-Might, Tom, dir. *Becoming You.* Documentary. USA: Apple
TV+. 2020.

Damour, Lisa. *Untangled: Guiding Teenage Girls through the Seven
Transitions into Adulthood.* New York: Ballantine Books, 2016.

Ginsberg, Kenneth. "Treasuring Our Teens with Dr. Ken Ginsburg."
Interview by Liz Gumbinner. *Spawned Parenting.* Apple Podcasts. March 18, 2019. Audio. 35:14. https://podcasts.apple.com/
kg/podcast/spawned-parenting-podcast-kristen-liz-coolmom-
picks/id1002671438?i=1000432202724.

Ginsburg, Kenneth R, Ilana Ginsburg, and Talia Ginsburg. *Raising Kids to Thrive: Balancing Love with Expectations and Protection with Trust.* Elk Grove Village, Il: American Academy of Pediatrics, 2015.

Chapter 7

Niurka. *Supreme Influence: Change Your Life with the Power of the Language You Use.* New York: Harmony Books, 2013.

Rainey, Brooklyn. *One Trusted Adult: How to Build Strong Connections & Healthy Boundaries with Young People.* USA: Circle Talk, 2019. Kindle.

Chapter 8

Damour, Lisa. *Under Pressure: Confronting the Epidemic of Stress and Anxiety in Girls.* New York: Ballantine, 2020.

Fenton, Melissa. 2021. "Trying to Be 'Perfect' Is Killing Our Teens and We're to Blame." *Grown and Flown*, May 23, 2021. https://grownandflown.com/trying-perfect-killing-teens.

Ginsburg, Kenneth. "Treasuring Our Teens with Dr. Ken Ginsburg." Interview by Liz Gumbinner. *Spawned Parenting.* Apple Podcasts. March 18, 2019. Audio. 35:14. https://podcasts.apple.com/kg/podcast/spawned-parenting-podcast-kristen-liz-coolmompicks/id1002671438?i=1000432202724.

Sax, Leonard. *Why Gender Matters: What Parents and Teachers Need to Know about the Emerging Science of Sex Differences.* New York: Harmony Books, 2017.